COUNTRY DOUGHCRAFT

～ FOR YOUR HOME ～

COUNTRY DOUGHCRAFT

❧ FOR YOUR HOME ❧

Linda Rogers

Watson-Guptill Publications • New York

I would like to dedicate this book to my mother and father, Mary and Mick Mallin, in celebration of their golden wedding anniversary on September 20th 1997.

Page 2: Sunflowers and Daisies (page 58).

First published in the United States in 1988
by Watson-Guptill Publications,
a division of BPI Communications, Inc.,
1515 Broadway, New York, N.Y. 10036

Library of Congress Catalog Card Number:98-85200

ISBN 0-8230-0964-5

First published in the United Kindom in 1998
by David & Charles

Printed and bound in Great Britain by
Butler & Tanner Ltd, Frome and London

First printing, 1998

1 2 3 4 5 6 7 8 9/06 05 04 03 02 01 00 99 98

CONTENTS

INTRODUCTION

*W*hat now seems like a lifetime ago, I ventured along to my local village hall to see a demonstration of 'Salt Dough Sculpture'. Having never heard of this particular craft I was intrigued, and spent a wonderful evening learning all about doughcraft. I left that meeting totally inspired and now eight years later have a thriving business producing and selling doughcraft items, and am fortunate enough to have had the opportunity to write books on the subject. So beware! I am living proof that it can take over your life. It seems as though my trusty oven hasn't been switched off for years, and my kitchen is under a permanent cloud of flour!

The 'country look' has always been popular but never more so than in recent years. It is no longer necessary for you to own a rambling farmhouse or stately country pile to adopt a simple country style. The most modest of modern houses now can look absolutely charming with old pine furniture and farmhouse-type kitchen units. The current popularity of the American 'New England' look and simple Shaker designs has also been instrumental in putting together the projects for this book. In other words, Country Doughcraft is for everyone.

You need no special skills, tools, equipment or ingredients, and it is a very inexpensive hobby. Many of the projects featured are left natural in some part so that it is obvious that they are made from dough. It is also possible however to use salt dough as a substitute for clay, and once painted and varnished it is hard to distinguish the finished item from the kiln-fired and glazed alternative. This is a wonderful discovery for those of us who have always had a yearning to be potters, but found the idea too daunting!

Salt dough sculptures can often be personalised to make wonderful gifts, for example painting figures to look like somebody you know, or changing the style of a house to look like a particular building. You could focus on a friend's hobby or make models of their pets as a unique present, which will always be appreciated. Much of the history and folklore surrounding doughcraft is associated with giving, and a present of a hand-made dough sculpture traditionally brings good luck and prosperity to the recipient. You may well find however that you are so pleased with your works of art that you can't bear to part with them.

Dough sculpture really isn't difficult, so look through the pages of this book where I hope you will find some inspiration, and then head for the kitchen cupboard!

Opposite (from top to bottom): Milk Churns (page 90); Kissing Pigs (page 89) and Stone Cottage (page 24).

Chapter 1

GETTING
STARTED

SALT DOUGH

The ingredients for a basic salt dough are simply flour, salt and water.

Flour – this should be a good quality, all-purpose plain white flour. All brands of flour vary according to the quality of the wheat they were ground from. On the whole, the more expensive brands contain more starch which gives a stronger dough. Do not be tempted to use a strong flour produced especially for bread making as this has a high gluten content which makes the dough too elastic. This property is necessary if making bread, but as there is no yeast in salt dough this is not necessary, and salt dough made with strong flour will spring out of shape. Salt dough can be made with rye flour or wholemeal flour for a more rustic effect and a darker coloured dough, but it is not so smooth, and although worth experimenting with,

is not suitable for the projects in this book.

Salt – this needs to be a fine-grain table or cooking salt. The finer the grain, the smoother your dough will be. If you find that even after kneading and resting, your dough is still 'grainy' you can grind the salt down to a finer powder in a food processor before making the dough.

Water – slighty tepid water will help to give a smoother dough as it dissolves the grains of salt a little more quickly.

Optional Extras – there are recipes for salt dough containing such ingredients as cornflour, potato flour, oil, glycerine, wallpaper paste or PVA glue. These are supposed to make the dough more pliable or stronger or prevent mould. By all means experiment, but having tried them all I find the basic dough is the best.

PAINTS

You can use any type of paints for decorating your dough sculptures – from a children's paintbox, to household emulsion or car spray paint! All these certainly have their uses for creating different effects but generally I would recommend a water-based paint as you can wipe off any mistakes and it is much easier to clean the brushes.

The most versatile paints are gouache paints which are available in tubes from art and craft shops in a huge variety of colours, including metallics. This means that if you are not confident of mixing your own colours you can almost

certainly buy the colour you want. Gouache generally gives a stronger, more opaque colour than water colour paints which have a more delicate transparent quality and can be used effectively to give a subtle coloured wash to the natural dough.

Acrylic paints are also water-based, but are more difficult to use as they are very quick drying, so removing mistakes is tricky as the paint dries to a hard, plastic-like waterproof finish. Unless you have a special 'wet' palette it can also be very wasteful using these paints, as any surplus left on the palette will dry quickly and cannot be re-used.

VARNISH

The best type of varnish to use is an ordinary wood varnish available from your local DIY (hardware, or home builder's supply) store . The non-drip ones provide an excellent base coat. These are available in a number of different finishes and colours. Yacht varnish is also extremely good for doughcraft as it produces a very tough, high gloss, waterproof finish which is ideal for a top coat, but it does tend to soak into the dough a little if used as a base coat. Never

use a water-based acrylic varnish. These 'quick-drying' varieties soak into the dough and will smudge any paint you have applied.

There are 'special effect' finishes that are available such as a crackle glaze for an antique effect. At least one of these substances is water based and although they produce marvellous finishes on furniture and paintings, they are unfortunately not successful on doughcraft.

The tools and equipment for dough making are readily found in the kitchen, and very few specialist items are required.

Large mixing bowl
Straight-sided cup
Sharp knife
Rolling pin
Baking sheets – the salt in the dough will quickly attack the surface of metal baking trays causing them to rust; it will also very rapidly remove the surface from the non-stick variety. Stove enamelled or aluminium trays are resistant to the effects of the salt, but are rather expensive to buy. The best solution is probably to buy some cheap baking sheets and keep them just for your dough modelling (a little rust colour on the backs of your models won't hurt). Greasing the trays lightly as you would do for normal baking, although not necessary, will help them last longer, or you can line them with baking parchment. Greaseproof paper or tin foil are *not* suitable as they will stick fast to the backs of your models.

Round trays – such as pizza trays are preferable to baking sheets if making a garland or circular model, as it is notoriously difficult to produce a good circle on a square tray!

Modelling tools – no special modelling tools are required but you will need some thin wooden skewers (the sort used for barbecuing kebabs) or cocktail sticks. The skewers are stronger than wooden cocktail sticks and their extra length makes them easier to handle. Other items such as scissors, forks, round-bladed knives, drinking straws, paper-clips, cake decorating equipment, and cookie cutters will also come in handy.
Note: "Sugarcraft tools" include cake decorating equipment and speciality cookie cutters and presses.

Cutters – all shapes and sizes of cutters are useful, particularly leaf and flower shapes. There are some marvellous leaf cutters available from cake decorating shops, which will mark veins on the leaves at the same time as pressing out the shape.

These are not absolutely necessary however, as it is always possible to mould leaves and flowers by hand, or cut out the shapes with a knife.

Potato ricer or garlic press – these items are particularly useful as they make the most wonderful grass or hair, by extruding long strands of dough through the holes. For the uninitiated, a potato ricer is rather like a giant garlic press, designed for mashing potatoes. It has the advantage of holding much more dough than a garlic press thus making the job a lot less labour intensive. Potato ricers are also available with different sized plates that fit into the base, enabling you to produce strands of dough of different thickness. They are available from good housewares stores.

Brushes – you will need several brushes for the different stages in making your models. First, a small pastry brush is needed for wetting the dough as you assemble the pieces. Second, you will need some artists' paintbrushes. The best type are synthetic ones as they are much harder wearing than natural fibres, and salt dough is tough on brushes! They are also not as soft as sable brushes which makes them easier to use. Although they are quite expensive it is worth investing in three different sizes, a No 4 round brush for fine work, a No 6 for general painting and a No 8 for larger areas. These will last you a long time and having the right brush for each job makes the work easier. Lastly you will need a decorator's brush for applying the varnish. A 50mm (2in) brush is ideal and buying a good quality one will ensure that the bristles don't fall out and stick to your work.

Paper-clips – different sizes will be needed for making hangers.

Cloves and black-headed map pins – are invaluable for stalks, eyes and noses.

MAKING DOUGH

The simplest way to measure out the basic ingredients for salt dough is by volume rather than weight. The ratio of ingredients is two parts flour to one part salt and one part water. Use a straight-sided cup to measure with. A good quantity of dough to start with would be:

4 cups flour
2 cups salt
2 cups water

Mix the flour and salt together well in your mixing bowl and then add the water, remembering that the salt dissolves better if the chill is taken off the water. Do not add quite all the water at this stage, as different brands of flour will not absorb the same amount of liquid, and the rest can be added if the dough is too dry. Using a round-bladed knife, mix the water in well and then turn out the dough and knead thoroughly on your work surface.

Kneading is very important, as the more your dough is kneaded the smoother it will be, and the warmth of your hands helps to dissolve the grains of salt. You should be able to tell at this stage if the consistency of the dough is right. It should be soft enough to mould readily (try rolling a ball in the palm of your hand), and yet firm enough to hold its shape. If it crumbles as you try to mould it, it is too dry so add a little water (it may be sufficient to simply wet your hands and re-knead the dough). If the dough sticks to your hands it is too wet, so you will need to add more flour. Having kneaded the dough for at least five minutes, it will benefit from a short rest (no more than half an hour), covered with a plastic bag to prevent a dry skin forming. **Storing uncooked dough** – Once your dough has been made for a couple of hours, the consistency will start to deteriorate, as it attracts moisture from the atmosphere and becomes sticky. If you do need to leave it for a while, cover with a plastic bag as when resting, but check it before you begin again. If it feels at all sticky, it is generally best to make a fresh batch. If you leave dough for any length of time the colour when baked is slightly darker, so it is not wise to use old and fresh dough in the same model as it will be two-tone!

MAKING MODELS

Specific instructions are given with each project but there are a few points common to all. Firstly, check that your dough is the correct consistency. When modelling with your hands, there is no need to flour your hands as the dough will not stick to them. Use flour though if rolling out with a rolling pin. Work directly on to your baking sheet as your model will distort if you make it on a work surface and then try to move it. When assembling your models, dampen the relevant area slightly with a little water to join together the parts. Too much water will produce a slippery surface and the pieces will tend to slide around. You will find that you need to wash your hands frequently when working with salt dough, so it helps to work near a sink.

Finally, salt dough is heavy and relatively soft, and if you try to make a model that stands up, it is likely to collapse or sink down into itself. To prevent this use something as a frame to build your model round: this can be a scrunched-up piece of tin foil or a cardboard toilet roll centre, or some wire netting. The same applies if any part of your model needs support during cooking. A ball of tin foil placed underneath the relevant part will support it and can be removed once baking is complete.

LAMINATING TECHNIQUE

This is a very successful way of preventing cracks from appearing in the larger models.

To laminate dough, cut a piece of nylon dressmaker's netting to the shape of your plaque. Roll out the dough to twice the size you need and brush with water. Lay the netting over one half of the dough and fold the other half over the top, re-rolling so that the netting is well sandwiched between the two layers of dough. Trim to shape with a sharp knife.

Templates can be very useful in providing you with shapes for doughcraft designs, allowing you to achieve the outline you want, and to repeat the design. Actual size templates for some of the projects in this book have been provided (see pages 118–127). To use, simply trace or photocopy the template on to thin card. Cut out the shape, lay lightly on top of the rolled-out dough and cut around the outline using a sharp knife.

Templates may also be easily enlarged or reduced by photocopier to make larger or smaller models. Remember that if you do this the amount of dough needed for the project will need to be adjusted accordingly.

MAKING A HANGER

Many pieces of doughcraft are designed to hang on the wall but it is not a good idea to do this without a special hanger. Salt dough is heavy and it puts too much strain on the supporting part which may break. There are several suitable ways of making a hanger. Lengths of ribbon, string or raffia can be threaded through for an attractive finish.

1 Making a hole in the dough
This method is the most suitable hanger for thin, flat models. Use a large plastic drinking straw as a miniature cutter to cut a hole in your model. If you simply poke a hole with a skewer without actually removing any of the dough, the hole will close up again on baking. It is possible to drill through the cooked dough very carefully using a small drill bit. Don't forget to varnish inside the hole.

2 Using paper-clips
This is the easiest and most successful method of making a hanger, but is not suitable for thin models as it will distort the shape. Make sure that you use the largest paper-clip possible for the size of the model you are making and push it well down into the dough so that the end with the double loop is buried. As the dough cooks it will rise slightly and mould itself around the paper-clip.

3 Using string or wire
A piece of string or twisted wire can be incorporated into your model when you are making it. Using string is quite difficult as you need to tie a knot, making a loop, and bury the knot well into the dough. You cannot push the string into the model, but need to build your piece up around it. A piece of wire with the ends twisted into a loop can be used in the same way as a paper-clip, but is not as strong. Don't use wire with open ends, such as hairpins as there is nothing to anchor in the dough and the ends will probably pull out. It is not a good idea to glue wire into holes drilled in the back of your model after baking, as dough is very heavy and not all glues can be relied upon.

BAKING DOUGH

Baking doughcraft is really a drying out process and takes several hours at a low temperature. Salt dough should be baked at between 100–120°C (200–250°F/Gas Mark ¼–½), slightly lower in a fan-assisted oven. Thin, flat models should be cooked at the lower end of the scale, as the heat will penetrate them more rapidly and may cause the model to rise and bubble. Larger, thicker models with a smooth surface should also be started off at a lower temperature, which can be increased after a few hours when the outside has set hard. With projects like the kissing pigs (see page 84) any rising is exaggerated and large cracks can appear around the base of the model. As a general rule of thumb dough should be cooked for one hour for every 6mm (¼in) thickness.

When cooked the dough will be golden brown and lift easily from the tray giving a hollow sound when tapped smartly on the back. If it is stuck to the tray or gives a dull sound when tapped, it is not ready and should be returned to the oven. As long as the temperature does not exceed 120°C (250°F/Gas mark ½) the dough will not burn.

Make sure your model is thoroughly cooked and dried out to the centre, as any remaining moisture will either continue to dry out after cooking and cause the piece to shrink and crack, or, once varnished, will be trapped and cause softening.

Every oven is different and once you have made a few models you will soon discover the best temperature within the above range. It is also worth experimenting with moving shelves around, as different parts of the oven cook at different speeds, so cooking times will vary. With some of the larger models you may find it convenient to bake your dough overnight. If you are worried about leaving it for so long you can always lower the temperature a little to compensate.

It is possible to air-dry salt dough, although I would not recommend it. You will need to leave your model somewhere warm and dry for several weeks. Dried in this way your model will remain white in colour and will never be as strong as when baked.

The other modern alternative is to microwave your dough. Again this is *not* a cooking method that I could recommend. Your dough will remain pale in colour, unless you over-cook it, in which case it will turn black almost immediately!

PAINTING DOUGH

Before you begin to paint your dough model, ensure that it is absolutely cold. If you try to paint while there is still any heat in it, the paint will dry immediately and will be patchy. The paint may also craze, as it will if applied too thickly. For obvious reasons ensure that one colour is dry before painting next to it with another colour.

Colours can be varied according to the thickness of the paint used. For more subtle colours, thin down the paint with water, whilst brighter, bolder colours are achieved with thicker paint. If you are using water colours or gouache and make a mistake while painting, simply wipe off the offending paint with a damp cloth and start again. A wide variety of colours are available straight from the tube, but if you do not wish to buy too many, any colour can be mixed from a few primary colours plus black and white. I have always found 'permanent white' and 'ivory black' to be the best.

Some people prefer not to paint their models at all but to leave them with a natural finish. If this is the case, the appearance can be enhanced by eggwashing the piece before you bake it. Make sure that you cover your model completely and evenly with the egg, as any missed bits will show as a lighter colour, and any places where the eggwash is too thick will come up darker. For those preferring a natural look, a wash of very thin brown paint applied after baking will give a sepia effect to the finished model.

VARNISHING DOUGH

This is the most important part in doughcraft, as the varnish protects the finished dough article from the atmosphere. Unvarnished, your piece will soon soften if left exposed. Make absolutely sure that the paint is completely dry, and indeed that the model is completely dried out before varnishing. Any remaining moisture will be trapped once the varnish is applied and will cause softening.

Apply varnish with a good quality brush to avoid losing bristles. If using a stained varnish for an antique effect, apply as a base coat and rub on with a soft cloth for a thinner, more even covering. Ensure that every nook and cranny is well covered as even a pinhead-sized hole in the varnish will allow moisture through. Give your models at least two, but preferably three coats of varnish on both sides for maximum protection. The ideal combination is two coats of non-drip varnish followed by a top coat of yacht varnish. It helps to wear disposable gloves when varnishing, and it is best to varnish your piece all over (front and back) in one go. Several thin coats are better than fewer thick ones for avoiding drips and runs.

A wire rack such as a cake rack is excellent for leaving the varnish to dry, and you will need to leave approximately six hours between coats. If, however you don't have a suitable rack and you find it necessary to varnish one side at a time, place the dough on a plastic sheet to dry, as the varnish will stick to paper. Beware, however, of colour or print on the plastic as the varnish may cause it to lift off and stain your model.

CARE OF DOUGH MODELS

Under normal household conditions your dough models should keep for many years. If kept in an excessively damp atmosphere it may soften, but it can be re-hardened (see Troubleshooting page 14). To clean it, simply dust or wipe with a damp cloth, but do not immerse in water. You may find that a new coat of varnish will brighten an old dough piece up. Do not place in direct steam such as near a kettle or in a steamy bathroom as this may affect the varnish. Avoid direct sunlight as it will fade the paint. If you need to store doughcraft items, wrap well in bubble wrap and keep dry.

*H*aving mastered the basic techniques, you are all set to start creating your own beautiful models. If things should go wrong, don't despair – most problems are easily solved. The following is a list of the more common faults that may occur.

RISING, BLISTERING DOUGH

If the dough rises and forms bubbles during baking, this is an indication that either the dough was too wet or the oven too hot – or both! If the dough is still soft enough, press gently back into shape and reduce the temperature of the oven for the remainder of the cooking time. As this fault is more common with thin, flat models it may be possible to weight the offending part down by covering with a folded tea towel and placing a cooking weight or similar heavy object on top of the tea towel. Don't worry the tea towel won't catch fire!

For future reference, if the dough is too soft it will not hold its shape well and detail will be lost. If the problem is that the oven is too hot, the dough will start to brown slightly before it hardens. Look out for loss of detail or browning and this should help you decide what caused the fault and how to avoid it next time.

CRACKS

It appears that cracks which appear during or after baking are an occupational hazard of doughcraft. Although they are rare, it is sometimes almost impossible to avoid them. They occur most frequently in the larger models and using the laminating technique (see page 11) definitely reduces the incidence of cracks. Cracks on the reverse of your model are incidental to the baking process and are not detrimental, although they can be reduced by cooking at lower temperatures, particularly with thicker models.

The cracks that are particularly upsetting are the hairline cracks that appear from nowhere after baking is complete, often making a loud noise as they do so. Changes of temperature cause slight expansion and contraction in the dough, causing stresses which can lead to cracking. Sometimes this happens during the cooling process, particularly with the larger pieces, so it helps to

cool them very slowly, leaving them in the oven after switching off until completely cool.

If cracks do appear after baking they can be filled with a little fresh dough using the same principle as a filler on plaster. Leave the filler dough to dry out naturally in a warm room and, when dry, touch up with fresh paint and varnish. It is not advisable to re-bake, as the changes in temperature may cause another crack.

SOFTENING DOUGH

If atmospheric conditions are exceptionally humid, or your dough models are kept in a particularly damp place, they may become soft and spongy. They can be re-hardened by placing them on a radiator for several days. It is a good idea to give them another coat of varnish once they are completely dry. Damp is the only thing that will cause softening, and if you are sure that your models are not being kept in a damp atmosphere, then it may be that they were not completely cooked and moisture was trapped inside when you varnished. If this is so, then the same remedy applies, but the process of re-hardening will take weeks.

REPAIRING BREAKS

Salt dough is fairly durable but may break if dropped. If the break is clean, it can be successfully repaired with a strong glue such as Superglue or a PVA craft glue. If the damage is small, such as an ear knocked off and lost, or part of a leaf crumbled away, the offending part can be restructured using fresh dough. It is better to allow the repair to air dry naturally in a warm place for a few days, rather than returning to the oven which will discolour the varnish and may cause cracking. When it is hard it is a simple matter to re-touch with paint and varnish.

FLAKING VARNISH

This is caused by the model being exposed to damp or steam. If it occurs, the appearance of your sculpture can be improved by rubbing away the flaking varnish gently with a very fine piece of emery paper, taking care not to scratch the paint underneath. Then give two coats of fresh varnish and re-hang in a different location.

*M*astering certain basic shapes and techniques will allow you not only to produce the wide variety of designs in this book but also to create your own original models. Begin by rolling out the dough exactly as you would pastry, using a floured rolling pin on a lightly floured surface. Practice cutting flat shapes with a knife or cutters, and using the templates at the back of the book (see pages 118–127). The other shapes illustrated in this section are moulded by hand.

FRUIT

STRAWBERRIES
A small ball of dough, moulded to a point at one end and marked with a cocktail stick to give the effect of seeds. For the stalk use a deseeded clove, or a small star-shaped leaf cut from a flattened ball of dough, and anchor this in place with a clove stalk.

PEAR
A ball of dough elongated and narrowed at one end, with a clove stalk as in the apple, and a small leaf added.

GRAPES
Small balls of dough combined in a slight 'S' shape. Add leaf, stalk and vine – a spaghetti-shaped piece of dough laid on top and twisted.

APPLE
A simple ball of dough with a clove pushed in 'head-first' to make a stalk. A leaf can be added if required.

PLUMS
A small oval-shaped ball of dough, with a crease added down one side using a cocktail stick, and a hole pressed in the top. Size, shape and colour can be varied to produce cherries, peaches, apricots etc.

ORANGE
A ball of dough pitted with the blunt end of a bamboo skewer, or rolled on the zesting part of a cheese grater to give the orange peel effect. A clove with the seed broken off is used as the stalk.

BANANAS
Are best avoided!

CAULIFLOWER

As for the cabbage, but with a larger centre ball and fewer outside leaves. Pit the centre with the blunt end of a bamboo skewer, then, using the point, or a cocktail stick, divide the cauliflower head into flowers.

POTATO

Roll oval-shaped balls of dough and, using the blunt end of a wooden skewer, mark three or four 'eyes' in each potato. They will look very realistic when painted.

GREEN BEANS

Roll a long thin piece of dough, thinner at the very end, and flatten roughly, making indentations with your thumb at regular intervals.

LEEK

Flatten a long sausage of dough at one end, and then cut off that end in a 'V' shape. Add roots made from dough extruded through a garlic press and mark the leaves with a sharp knife. The best effect can be seen when painted.

TOMATOES

Make a small ball of dough, adding a star-shaped leaf held with a clove 'stalk' as for a strawberry.

CARROT

Roll a long pointed piece of dough, and then, using a very small circular cutter or the end of a straw, mark a ring in the top of the carrot. Using a sharp knife, mark fine ridges across the carrot all the way down it.

MUSHROOMS

Roll a small ball of dough, and using a very small circular cutter or the end of a straw, press about halfway into the dough to form the stalk.

CABBAGE

Using a ball of dough for the centre of the cabbage, build up the outside leaves in the same way as you add the petals when making a rose.

ASPARAGUS

Roll a bundle of spear-shaped pieces of dough and snip the ends and shafts with nail scissors.

DAISY SHAPE
This can be made from thinly rolled out dough using a small sugarcraft cutter, or moulded from a flattened ball of dough with the edges drawn up with a cocktail stick. Push a hole in the centre.

ROSE
The centre of the rose is made from a flattened ball of dough rolled up to form a tight bud. The flower is built up to the required shape by rolling successive flattened dough petals around the centre bud.

USING CUTTERS
This method is especially useful for leaves of complicated shape such as holly or ivy. Roll dough out thinly with a rolling pin and, after using the cutter, mark veins with a cocktail stick.

PINCHED LEAVES
A stylised leaf suitable for trees or hedges can be made by pinching a piece of dough between thumb and forefinger, then breaking it off. Make a number, then pile them on top of each other.

CUT LEAVES
A simple leaf can be made from a rolled out piece of dough, by cutting it into long narrow strips and then cutting these into diamond shapes. Veins are marked with a cocktail stick.

MOULDED LEAVES
These can be made from a flattened ball of dough pinched to a point at one end. The sides can be drawn up with a skewer if desired to give more of an oak leaf effect. Mark veins as before.

TREES
Tree trunks can be formed by the following methods, with leaves and fruit added.

A long roll of dough, flattened slightly, and the bark marked with a knife.

As left, with branches formed by making two cuts down from the top of the trunk.

ough baskets can be fashioned in many different ways, simple or more complex, and be either wall-hanging or free-standing.

The projects in this book use basic flat wall-hanging baskets in different shapes and with different types of weave.

A much finer 'weave' can be created using a fork to make the evenly spaced lines across the basket, with a wooden skewer drawn down over them to form the vertical lines.

A simple basket-weave pattern can be created using a wooden skewer to press lines into the dough.

This woven basket is made by laying narrow strips of thinly rolled dough diagonally across the base, then laying shorter pieces across the top, to give the woven effect. Continue building up this pattern as shown until the basket is covered then finish off the top and bottom edges with twists.

The lattice work effect of this basket is created by laying thin snakes of dough diagonally across the base in both directions and then finishing with twisted snakes of dough as shown.

EXTRUDING AND SNIPPING

A small pair of scissors can be used to snip dough to form ears of wheat, pine trees or flower petals. This technique is also good for hedgehog spines or feathers on birds.

Extruded dough, pushed through a potato ricer, or garlic press, makes wonderful 'hair'. This can be cut off with a knife to different lengths to make grass, hair, sheep's wool, manes and tails, etc.

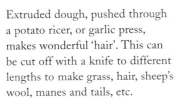

*T*he basic structure of any figure should be kept simple with stylised features. It is very difficult to fashion realistic-looking hands and features, so it is best not to try! Here is the basic frame to which you can add clothing or alter the stance for each individual figure.

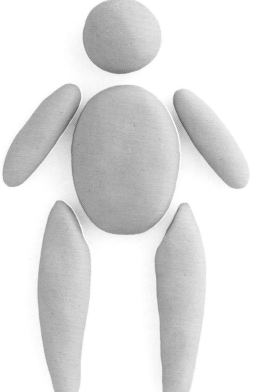

HEAD AND BODY
Create the trunk and head from two balls of dough, the larger for the body being slightly flattened.

ARMS AND LEGS
Add legs to the body and arms to the sides of the trunk. The thickness of the limbs can be varied to accommodate clothing. For a man wearing trousers, simply make the legs thicker rather than trying to add trousers on top of thin legs. The same applies to long sleeves.

FEATURES
It is best to paint features for the most detail, although you can add a small button nose and highlight eyes and mouth by poking a hole with a bamboo skewer, to be defined with paint later.

HANDS AND FEET
These, in their simplest form, are balls and sausages of dough added to the limbs.

HAIR
By far the most satisfactory way of producing hair is to use dough extruded through a garlic press or potato ricer. Lengths of spaghetti dough can be produced in this way and fashioned into any style you like.

Chapter 2

HOME
SWEET HOME

*T*here is an old saying that 'The road to a friend's house is never long'. This simple plaque with the little road leading up to the cottage, is an ideal project for a beginner. It would be a lovely gift for a friend, perhaps for a new home, or alternatively would provide a warm welcome in a guest room.

- *3 cups flour made into dough (see page 11)*
- *A piece of nylon netting 17.5cm (7in) square*
- *Knife*
- *Plastic drinking straw*
- *Potato ricer or garlic press*
- *1m (1yd) gingham ribbon about 2.5cm (1in) wide*
- *PVA glue*
- *String*
- *Paint*
- *Varnish*

1 Roll out your dough to an oblong shape at least 20 x 40cm (8 x 16in), and approximately 6mm (¼in) thick. Using the laminating technique (see page 11), fold over the dough and cut into a 17.5cm (7in) square. Lightly mark a 2.5cm (1in) border all around the edge with a knife, and using the plastic straw cut a hole in each top corner.

2 Make the sun by flattening several small, long, thin triangles of dough, positioning them just inside the border in the top left-hand corner of the plaque, radiating outwards and leaving a circular space in the centre. Flatten a small ball of dough and place in the centre on top of the rays. Place another long, thin flattened triangle of dough in the top right-hand corner and using a small pair of scissors create a pine tree (see page 17).

3 Roll out a small piece of dough to 6mm (¼in) thick and using the trace-off template on page 118

cut out the cottage shape and place on the plaque as shown. Mark the shape of the doorway and add vertical lines for the planks of the door. Outline the doorway with a very thin snake of dough, and add a small ball of dough for the doorknob. The roof is made from a flattened sausage of dough, bent around the top of the house and flattened.

4 Mark the roadway with a knife and add a few clumps of extruded dough grass (see page 18) either side of the roadway. Finally add a bush made from small pieces of pinched dough (see page 17) with small flowers made either with a blossom cutter or by hand (see page 17).

5 Bake, paint as desired and varnish according to the instructions in Basic Techniques. When the varnish is dry, glue the ribbon around the border, mitring the corners neatly. Make holes in the corners of the ribbon where there are holes in the dough, and thread the string through for a hanger.

STONE COTTAGE

*T*his rather dismal looking stone cottage is typical of many found around the country. If you prefer a brighter, more cheerful effect, this can easily be achieved by baking the plaque a slightly lighter colour, and adding a few flowers, possibly in the form of window boxes, or in the border along the front edge.

- *4 cups flour made into dough (see page 11)*
- *A piece of nylon netting about 30cm (12in) square*
- *Knife*
- *Wooden skewer or cocktail stick*
- *Potato ricer or garlic press*
- *Extra large paper-clip*
- *Paint*
- *Varnish*

1 Roll out two-thirds of your dough to an oblong shape approximately 45 x 20cm (18 x 8in) and 6mm (¼in) thick. Cut the netting to shape and using the laminating technique (see page 11) fold over the dough. Using the trace-off template on page 118, cut out the plaque shape with a sharp knife.

2 Roll out the remainder of your dough to 6mm (¼in) thick, and using the template on page 118, cut out the shape of the cottage and lay onto the plaque. Make the roof tiles by overlapping strips of very thinly rolled dough across the roof, marking the tiles with a knife. Add a chimney pot made from two squares of dough as shown.

3 Mark the positions of the door and windows with a knife and outline with strips of thinly rolled dough made from the trimmings. Mark the door planks with a knife, and add a small ball of dough for the door knob. Next place thinly rolled snakes of dough across the base of the roof tiles and running up the side of the cottage for guttering and drainpipe.

4 Mark the stone effect on the walls using a wooden skewer. You will find it easier to push the blunt end of the skewer repeatedly into the dough rather than drag the pointed end across the dough which can easily distort the shape.

5 Add a tree growing up the side of the cottage using the 'pinched' leaf technique (see page 17), and a base of grass made from dough extruded through the garlic press or potato ricer.

6 Push a very large paper-clip into the centre top for hanging and bake as instructed in Basic Techniques. Paint your cottage as desired, not forgetting to paint in the window details with white paint on top of thoroughly dry dark grey or black. Varnish as instructed in Basic Techniques.

*T*his charming 'chocolate box' cottage is quite simple to make, but you really need a potato ricer as the thatch becomes a very long-winded job with a garlic press. Change the wisteria to roses or other flowers if you prefer by painting on different shapes and colours.

- *3 cups flour made into dough (see page 11)*
- *Knife*
- *Potato ricer (preferably) or garlic press*
- *2 medium paper-clips*
- *Paint*
- *Varnish*

1 Using the trace-off template on page 119, cut the shape of the cottage from dough rolled out to 1cm (³⁄₈in) thick. With a knife mark the position of the door and windows and score lines in the door to create the effect of wooden planks. Roll some very thin snakes of dough and use to outline the window frames and create the trellis either side of the door as shown. A small loop for the door knocker can be added at the same time.

2 Using the potato ricer extrude long lengths of dough and cover the roof of the cottage, varying the length of the 'thatch' to give a curved effect above the windows. Add much shorter lengths over the front door. The top of the thatch is cut from dough rolled out to 3mm (¹⁄₈in) using the template (see page 119) as a guide. Place this in position and with a knife score vertical lines and a criss-cross pattern as shown in the photograph.

3 Cut the chimney stack from dough rolled out to 6mm (¹⁄₄in) thick, using the template on page 119 and lay in position on your cottage. You will need to flatten the thatch slightly underneath the chimney stack so that it doesn't bulge. Roll a very thin snake of dough and place some strips of this growing up the stack to use as stems when painting the flowers later.

4 Following the instructions on page 17, make three trees of different sizes and place them against the end wall of the cottage. Finally, add grass around the bottom of the cottage by extruding lengths through a garlic press. Put into place, leaving a gap in front of the door.

5 Push a medium paper-clip for hanging into the top of the cottage, one at each end of the roof. Bake, paint as desired and varnish as instructed in Basic Techniques.

*T*his row of different houses is typical of those found in any village. They range from a tiny red brick cottage to an imposing three-storey building. You could make the houses individually, changing details to personalise them.

- *2 cups flour made into dough (see page 11)*
- *Knife*
- *2 medium paper-clips*
- *Paint*
- *Varnish*

1 Roll out your dough to 6mm (¼in) thick and using the trace-off template on page 120, cut out the base. With a knife, gently mark the divisions between the houses. It is best to decorate each house individually using the dough trimmings.

2 Beginning with the cottage on the left, lay some overlapping strips of thinly rolled out dough across the roof area. Add two small, square chimney pots. Mark the door and windows with a knife and outline with very thin snakes of dough. Mark the door planks and brickwork with a knife and add a tiny doorknob.

3 The raised detail on the white house is made by laying a strip of rolled out dough with a pointed top on the relevant part of the house. Mark the door and windows with a knife and outline with very thin snakes of dough. Add a tiny loop for the knocker. Place a small, square chimney pot at the

top, and make several roof tiles by flattening small balls of dough. Lay these in overlapping rows across the roof and above the front door.

4 The large three-storey building is simply decorated with window shutters. Mark the windows with a knife and place small strips of very thinly rolled dough down either side of each window. Mark vertical lines on the shutters. Add two small chimney pots.

5 The little white cottage roof is made by cutting small squares of thinly rolled out dough and laying them in overlapping rows. Mark the door and windows with a knife and outline with very thin snakes of dough, adding a tiny, oblong letter box. Mark a small heart above the door if you wish.

6 Finally, add one or more small trees in front of the houses (see Creating Basic Shapes page 17). Push a paper-clip into the top of each end of your model for hanging and bake. Paint as desired (not forgetting the window detail) and varnish as instructed in Basic Techniques.

These two simple projects are complementary and would be easy projects for the beginner. The country quilt illustrates an interesting use of doughcraft incorporated with other materials.

For the dovecote:

- *2 cups flour made into dough (see page 11)*
- *Knife*
- *Small scissors*
- *Plastic drinking straw*
- *Raffia*
- *String*
- *Paint*
- *Varnish*

For the country quilt:

- *1 cup flour made into dough (see page 11)*
- *Sharp knife*
- *Wooden skewer or cocktail stick*
- *Button thread*
- *Assorted pieces of coloured paper*
- *Polyvinyl acetate (PVA) glue*
- *20cm (8in) square picture frame with mountboard but no glass*
- *Paint*
- *Varnish*

FOR THE DOVECOTE:

1 Roll out your dough to 6mm (¼in) thick and using the templates on page 120, cut out the dovecote shape and three heart shapes.

2 Add the roof, made from flattened sausages of dough cut to fit the apex. With the drinking straw cut holes in the top of each of the heart shapes, and in the centre bottom and centre top of the dovecote, being sure to go right through the roof and base. Cut a round hole 2.5cm (1in) in the centre of the dovecote using a cutter if you have one, alternatively, cut round the edge of a coin.

3 Make three little birds by moulding small balls of dough into a bird shape as shown, snipping the wing with a pair of scissors. A very small triangle of dough is added for the beak, and the eye is marked with a skewer. Place the birds in position on the dovecote, and add a small heart shape at the apex of the roof as shown in the photograph.

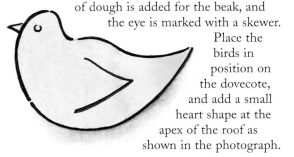

4 Bake, paint as desired and varnish as instructed in Basic Techniques. Thread a loop of string through the top for hanging and attach the three hearts to the bottom with different lengths of string. Tie a raffia bow around the strings where they join the dovecote.

FOR THE COUNTRY QUILT:

5 Make sixteen buttons. These are cut from thinly rolled out dough using cutters or a knife in a variety of different shapes as shown. Using a wooden skewer, poke two holes in the centre of each button, making sure that you have gone right through the dough otherwise the holes will close up on cooking.

6 Bake, paint and varnish as instructed in Basic Techniques. When thoroughly dry, thread a length of button thread through each (this is easiest with a needle) and tie into a knot on top of the button.

7 Cut or tear a square of paper to fit just inside your picture frame, then make sixteen smaller squares of different coloured paper. Tear paper along a ruler to get a straight edge. Arrange your small squares of paper on the large square and then place your buttons on top of the small paper squares. When you are completely satisfied with the arrangement, glue the whole lot into place within the picture frame.

*T*his simple but charming plaque is reminiscent of traditional needlework samplers but takes less time and effort to make.

- *4 cups flour made into dough (see page 11)*
- *A piece of nylon netting 15 x 20cm (6 x 8in)*
- *Knife*
- *Small heart-shaped cutter (optional)*
- *Large paper-clip*
- *Paint*
- *Varnish (satin and gloss)*

1 Roll out your dough to 6mm (¼in) thick and cut two pieces 15 x 20cm (6 x 8in). Using the laminating technique (see page 12) sandwich the netting between the two pieces and trim up the edges. Cut four strips of dough 2.5cm (1in) wide for the frame. Lay these on top of your base around the edges, attaching with a little water. To mitre the corners neatly, lay one strip on top of the other and cut through both layers on the diagonal. Remove surplus dough from the end of each strip. Using a sharp knife, gently mark the frame of your picture to give a woodgrain effect.

2 Cut out the house shape and chimney, from a piece of very thinly rolled dough. Cut a triangle for the roof and place in position. Site the house in the picture centre. Mark door and windows with a knife and mark vertical lines on the door. Add a small ball of dough for the doorknob and outline the doorway with a very thin snake of dough. The detail on the windows is painted on later. If you have a small heart-shaped cutter, press it lightly into the roof to add decorative detail or mark it freehand with a knife or skewer.

3 For the tree trunks roll a small sausage of dough and flatten it. Cut a jagged edge at the bottom for roots, and make two cuts in the top of each to split the trunk into branches. Place these on either side of the house. Take ten small balls of dough and flatten them. Arrange five at the top of each tree for the leaves adding 'apples' in the centre of each.

4 Push a large paper-clip into the centre of your plaque, and bake as instructed in Basic Techniques. Paint your plaque as desired. I used a thin wash of dark brown paint for the frame, which highlights the woodgrain effect. When the paint is thoroughly dry, varnish your plaque. The model shown was given three coats of satin-finish varnish, and then when that was dry I brushed lightly over the raised areas with a gloss varnish for highlight.

These colourful fruits look good enough to eat and can be painted in many different colours to suit your decor. Cherries grow in colours ranging from yellow through red to black, and, using a little artistic licence, the grapes look quite acceptable in any of the following colours – purple, green, red, yellow, black, blue or burgundy.

- 2 cups flour made into dough (see page 11)
- Knife
- Wooden skewer or cocktail stick
- Wire for cherry stalks (such as brass-covered picture-hanging wire), or small piece of twig for grape stalk
- Large paper-clip
- Paint
- Varnish

1 For the grapes, take a piece of dough the size of a golf ball and form it into a cone shape. Flatten this in the palm of your hand to a triangular shape and place on the baking tray. Make two leaves of your choice (see page 17) and place at the top of the triangle.

2 Using the rest of your dough make a collection of small balls for the grapes. Lay these on to your base in structured groups as shown and continue building up until the base is completely covered and you are satisfied with the shape of the bunch. Roll a very thin snake of dough and lay this in a twisted shape over the top of the grapes to look like a length of vine. Push a small piece of twig into the top for the stalk.

3 For the bowl of cherries, use the template on page 121 and cut out the entire shape from dough rolled out to 1cm (³/₈in) thick. Roll out some more dough to 6mm (¹/₄in) thick, and cut just the bowl shape as indicated by the dotted line on the template. Wet the bottom half of your original piece and lay the bowl shape on top, trimming up the edges. With a knife, mark horizontal lines on the bowl to guide you when painting.

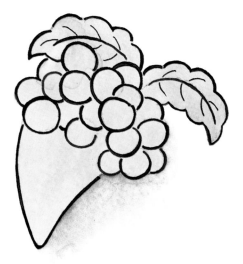

4 Roll balls of dough for the cherries and pile on the top section of your model. Make three or four leaves (see page 17) and tuck them between the cherries. Using a wooden skewer, push a hole into each of the cherries as shown. Cut a few pieces of wire about 5cm (2in) long and push into selected cherries to simulate stalks.

5 Push a large paper-clip into the top of your model for hanging, then bake, paint as desired and varnish as instructed in Basic Techniques.

PIES & COOKIES

These realistic pies and cookies look good enough to eat. By its very nature, salt dough is an ideal medium for making projects such as these, and the scope is virtually unlimited – from making something as simple as the little gingerbread people or a collection of bread rolls to the elaborate fruit tart shown here.

- 6 cups flour made into dough (see page 11)
- Knife
- Wooden skewer or cocktail stick
- Pie dish
- Flan dish
- Gingerbread cutters
- Small paper-clips
- Tin foil
- Paint
- Varnish

1 Starting with the gingerbread cookies, the most simple project, roll out a small amount of your dough to 6mm (¼in) thick and using the cutters press out the shapes. (If you do not have cutters simply make a template and cut round it.) Decorate your people with small balls of dough for eyes, noses and buttons, and finish off with very thin snakes of dough for the hair and clothes. The hearts are painted on after baking. Push a small paper-clip into the top of each head for hanging.

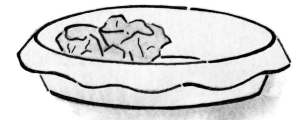

2 The large pie is made in exactly the same way as you would make a real one, but is filled with scrunched-up tin foil! Roll out your dough to 6mm (¼in) thick and line a lightly greased pie dish with the 'pastry'. Scrunch up several balls of tin foil to support the lid of the pie and then add the top, trimming to size and crimping the edges between your fingers for a decorative effect. Finish by adding a few leaves and berries in the centre.

Poke a hole in the centre to let out the 'steam' and stop the lid blowing off! Before baking brush with eggwash to give a lovely golden colour.

3 The fruit flan is also made exactly as you would a real one. Roll out your dough as before, and line a lightly greased flan dish with the 'pastry'. You will need to make a selection of fruit from your left-over dough and then arrange this in the flan. It is easier to stick to simple shapes such as the cherries and pineapple chunks that I have used. I made the apple slices by rolling a large ball of dough and cutting it into segments as you would a real apple. Bear in mind the finished colours when arranging your fruit so that the final effect is evenly balanced.

4 Bake, paint as desired and varnish as instructed in Basic Techniques.

These three models – teapot, coffee pot and kettle – are all made using the same basic construction, simply varying the shapes accordingly. The majority of the detail is painted on, in this case to mimic traditional folk art. You could of course paint the pots in any way, blue and white would be particularly effective.

- *2 cups flour made into dough (see page 11)*
- *Knife*
- *Wooden skewer or cocktail stick*
- *Medium paper-clip*
- *Paint*
- *Varnish*

1 For the teapot roll a ball of dough the size of an orange and then flatten it onto your baking tray with the palm of your hand. For the coffee pot and kettle, working with your hands rather than a rolling pin, try to mould a piece of dough of approximately the right shape, and about 1.5cm (⅝in) thick. Then, using the templates on page 127 as a guide, cut your model to exactly the right shape, rounding off the cut edges to give a spherical effect. Add a triangular lid to the coffee pot. With a skewer or knife, mark the line of the lids on the teapot and kettle. Add a knob to the top of each lid.

2 With a skewer or knife, mark any horizontal lines on the model that you may wish to paint, such as round the bases or lids, as a groove makes it much easier to get your line right when you are painting. Add thin snakes of dough around the bases of the pots as required, and around the join between pot and lid. A small hinge is added to the coffee pot lid.

3 The spouts are made by rolling a cone-shaped piece of dough in your hand and trimming the ends to the desired shape for pouring and attaching to your pot. With a little water attach the spout to the pot.

4 The handles are made by rolling a snake of dough and then flattening it with the palm of your hand. Trim it to the required length and then attach to the pot with a little water. The kettle handle has a strip of thinly rolled out dough wrapped around the top part to add extra detail.

5 Push a paper-clip into the top of the knob and bake as instructed in Basic Techniques. If you wish to decorate your pots elaborately there are many books available on traditional folk art. The hearts on the teapot are marked by lightly pressing with a small heart-shaped cutter and then following these lines when painting. The leaf border is also very simple and the effect is just as pleasing as the more elaborate designs. When your pots are painted, varnish them (see Basic Techniques).

This opulent basket of fruit is a more suitable project for those with some experience of dough modelling. However, don't be put off by this, as the design can easily be adapted to a much simpler one by omitting the woven effect of the basket and marking the basket weave with a skewer or fork instead.

- 4 cups flour made into dough (see page 11)
- Sharp knife
- Wooden skewer or cocktail stick
- Cloves
- Large paper-clip
- Paint
- Varnish

1 Using the trace-off template on page 122, cut the basket shape from a piece of dough rolled out to 1cm (⅜in) thick. Re-roll the trimmings to 6mm (¼in) thick and cut several strips approximately 1cm (⅜in) wide. Use these to create the basket weave (see page 18) over the lower half of your model as indicated on the template. Finish off the top and bottom edges of the basket with two thin snakes of dough twisted together as shown.

2 Make several leaves of your choice (see page 17) and lay them along the upper edge of your piece, leaving a couple of gaps for the grapes as shown in the photograph. I used sugarcraft cutters for the leaves in this particular project.

3 Make two each of the following fruits: apples, oranges, pears and lemons. These are made from golf ball-sized balls of dough, shaped accordingly for the pears and lemons. The surface of the oranges and lemons are pitted using the blunt end of a bamboo skewer. Arrange your fruits on the

basket as shown in the photograph. When arranging your fruit bear in mind the colour each piece is going to be when painted so that the colours are evenly balanced.

4 Roll lots of small balls of dough and pile these up to give the impression of bunches of grapes hanging over the basket. Add a couple of clusters of strawberries, made from small conical pieces of dough, and place a small leaf at the top of each pear.

5 Push cloves into your fruit for stalks – stalks upwards for apples and pears, and stalks down with the seed head broken off for oranges, lemons and strawberries. Finish off by filling in any gaps between the fruits with small blackcurrants, plums, leaves and strawberry flowers. Add a piece of twisted vine to the grapes if desired (see page 15).

6 Push a large paper-clip into the top for hanging. Bake, paint as desired and varnish as instructed in Basic Techniques.

This is a variation on the theme of the fruit basket in the last project. The basket weave is created in a different way, and the whole thing is given an antique effect. This is done by first painting the model then lightly rubbing over it with a satin-finish stained varnish, and finally highlighting the raised areas with a little gold paint on a dry brush. You will need to varnish as normal on top of this.

- *4 cups flour made into dough (see page 11)*
- *Knife*
- *Wooden skewer or cocktail stick*
- *Garlic press*
- *Cloves*
- *Medium paper-clip*
- *Paint*
- *Varnish*

1 Using the trace-off template on page 121, cut the basket from a piece of dough rolled out to 1cm (³⁄₈in) thick. Over the bottom half of the basket create a lattice-work basket weave (see page 18) and finish off with twisted ropes of dough at the top and bottom and a thinner rope about 2.5cm (1in) down from the top.

2 The vegetables are arranged over the top half of the basket as indicated by the dotted line on the template. To make the cabbage, start with a ball of dough the size of a cherry, and then keep adding leaves made from flattened balls of dough. These are built up around the edge of the cabbage, overlapping them as you go until it is the size you require. The cauliflower is made in the same way but starts with a larger ball of dough and only adding one layer of leaves around the edge. Mark the florets of the cauliflower with a skewer.

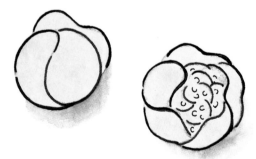

3 Potatoes are simply made from balls of dough with 'eyes' dotted in with the blunt end of a skewer. Button mushrooms are made from smaller balls of dough with a drinking straw pushed into the top to mark the stalk. The flat mushrooms are made by flattening a ball of dough, marking the gills with a knife and adding a small stalk.

4 Onions and beetroot are both made in the same way and then painted differently. Roll a ball of dough and then pinch up the top to form a point. Add some roots at the bottom, made using a garlic press (see page 18). Tomatoes are small balls of dough with a star-shaped stalk cut from a flattened piece of dough either with a sugarcraft cutter or a small pair of scissors, and held in place with a clove.

5 Peas and beans are simply snakes of dough. Carrots are moulded to shape by hand and then marked across with a knife. The circle at the top can be pressed in with a straw. The corn cobs are made by rolling a small sausage of dough and marking the kernels with a skewer. Two long leaves are added at the sides.

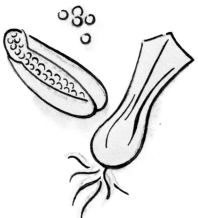

6 Finally, the leeks are made by rolling a sausage of dough and then flattening one end of it. Trim to shape as shown and mark the leaves with a knife. Add some roots at the bottom made with the garlic press.

7 Push a paper-clip into the top for hanging and bake, paint as desired and varnish as instructed in Basic Techniques.

I'm sure everybody would love an old pine dresser adorned with blue and white china in their kitchen, but for those of us who haven't the space, here's a smaller alternative!

- 3 cups flour made into dough (see page 11)
- A piece of nylon netting about 15 x 20cm (6 x 8in)
- Knife
- Wooden skewer or cocktail stick
- Blossom cutter (optional)
- Large paper-clip
- Paint
- Varnish (satin-finish stained, satin clear and gloss clear varnish)

1 Using the laminating technique (see page 11), roll out your dough to 6mm (¼in) thick. Cut out the shape of the dresser from this double layer using the template on page 122. Re-roll the trimmings and cut an oblong of dough to fit over the base, indicated by the dotted line on the template. Using a sharp knife, mark the outline of the drawers and cupboards as shown and add small balls of dough for knobs. Place balls of dough at the base of the dresser for feet.

2 Lay two thin snakes of dough horizontally across the dresser top for the shelves, and add a thin snake of dough round both the top and bottom edges of the dresser base. Following the templates, cut the sides and top of the dresser from thinly rolled out dough and place in position, attaching with a little water. Finally add another thin snake of dough around the very top edge.

3 Now add the china. Make any pieces you like and arrange them on the shelves. If you don't feel confident about making the more complicated pieces, a row of simple plates would look just as attractive, but vases are also very easy and the teapot is just a miniature version of the one on page 40. A vase of flowers or a bowl of fruit looks lovely on top of the base. If you haven't got a blossom cutter, small flowers can be made by flattening a tiny ball of dough and drawing up the edges with a skewer as shown, then pushing a hole in the centre.

4 Push a large paper-clip into the top for hanging and then bake as instructed in Basic Techniques. Once baked and cold, paint all the china plain white, then when dry add the blue decoration. Look for patterns to copy from magazines or books or even your own china, but if that is too difficult, stick to spots and stripes.

5 When the paint is completely dry, brush over the dresser with a very thin coat of stained varnish, avoiding the china. This gives a wood effect and highlights the cupboard and drawer markings. Give the whole model a coat of clear satin-finish varnish, and when dry, pick out the china with gloss varnish using a tiny paintbrush.

This jolly, plump farmer's wife with her hand-knitted sweater and flowery pinny would be at home in any kitchen. You could have a go at designing a jolly plump farmer to complement this cheerful figure.

- 2 cups flour made into dough (see page 11)
- Knife
- Wooden skewer or cocktail stick
- Garlic press
- Medium paper-clip
- Paint
- Varnish

1 Make the head, torso and legs of the figure (forgetting the arms for the moment), as instructed in Creating Basic Shapes (see page 19). Add two small, fat feet (the shoes are painted on after baking). Don't make your figure too fat at this stage as adding the clothes will add pounds!

2 The next step is to start to dress the figure. This is done just like real dressmaking, cutting the clothes to fit from very thinly rolled out dough. If you find it difficult to do this by eye, you can cut a pattern from waxed paper which is laid over the model and cut in situ. First position the skirt and then the body of the sweater (the arms are still not attached at this stage). Add a chunky roll neck made from a flattened sausage of dough, and mark the knitted effect with a knife or skewer.

3 Next add the apron. This is a semi-circle cut from a piece of very thinly rolled dough, with a narrow strip added for the waistband. The frill around the edge is another narrow strip, crinkled up a little as it is joined to the apron to give a gathered effect.

4 Make the arms using sausages of dough attached just below the neck of the sweater, adding little balls of dough for the hands. Mark the fingers with a knife, and mark the sleeves to match the sweater. Make the rolling pin from a long thin sausage of dough with a flattened ball pressed onto each end, and place across the body as shown, positioning the arm to hold the rolling pin.

5 Finally, add a little button nose and some hair made from dough extruded through a garlic press. You can style the hair in any way you want. The eyes and mouth are painted on after baking. Push a paper-clip into the top of the head for hanging.

6 Bake, paint as desired and varnish according to the instructions in Basic Techniques.

*T*his plaque featuring a country-style cooking range is reminiscent of the scene in many farmhouse kitchens. It is a fairly complicated piece to make but quite straightforward if taken step by step.

- *4 cups flour made into dough (see page 11)*
- *Piece of nylon netting 15 x 20cm (6 x 8in)*
- *Knife*
- *Wooden skewer or cocktail stick*
- *Large paper-clip*
- *Paint (including silver and copper)*
- *Varnish (satin and gloss)*

1 Using the laminating technique (see page 11) make a basic plaque from rolled out dough cut to the shape of the trace-off template on page 123. Build up the arched alcove by attaching strips of dough 2.5cm (1in) wide, rolled out to 6mm (¼in) thick, down both sides and round the top of the plaque. Across the bottom add a piece of thinly rolled out dough about 5cm (2in) deep. Mitre the corners by cutting through both thicknesses of dough and removing the surplus as shown.

2 With a knife or skewer mark the brickwork both inside the alcove and around the edges. Mark the floor into square tiles as shown above. Roll out some dough thinly and cut an oblong to fit into the bottom half of the alcove for the cooker. Lay this in place, then add three smaller oblongs for the doors, with tiny pieces of dough for handles and hinges. Roll a snake of dough and flatten it for the pipe running up from the centre of the cooker to the top of the alcove.

3 Add a small, flattened piece of dough for the closed lid on the hob and a flattened circle up against the wall for the open lid. Add a small

handle to both. Make two circular pans, hanging on thin handles from the top of the alcove, and fashion a miniature kettle to sit on the hob. The instructions for the kettle on page 40 may help you. Roll a thin snake of dough and lay across the top of the cooker, then cut out a tea-towel from very thinly rolled dough and hang over this bar.

4 The little basket is made by flattening a ball of dough and cutting to shape, marking the weave with a skewer and adding thin ropes of dough top and bottom. The wellies are a little tricky and have to be modelled by hand as best you can. A thin strip of dough added for the sole, and a small buckle on the side give a more realistic effect.

5 Push a large paper-clip into the top of the plaque and bake, then paint as desired and varnish as instructed in Basic Techniques. This model had two coats of satin varnish with the cooker picked out in gloss.

Chapter 4

THE
COTTAGE
GARDEN

LAVENDER BASKET

This plaque – an ideal decoration for any room – makes a charming alternative to the dried flower equivalent. You can almost smell the fragrance from the tightly packed stalks of lavender.

- *3 cups flour made into dough (see page 11)*
- *Sharp knife*
- *Potato ricer*
- *Large paper-clip*
- *Paint*
- *Varnish*
- *Natural raffia*

1 Roll out half the dough to 1cm (³/₈in) thick, and using the trace-off template on page 123, cut out the basic shape. Roll out some more dough to 6mm (¹/₄in) thick and cut into strips 1cm (³/₈in) wide. Following the instructions in Basic Techniques (see page 18) create a diagonally woven basket on the lower half of your model as indicated on the template.

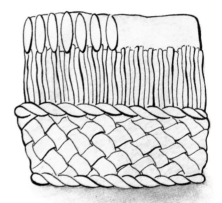

2 Using the potato ricer, extrude some long lengths of dough and lay these vertically on the top half of the model for the lavender stems. Make a rope from two thin snakes of dough twisted together and lay along the top edge of the basket to hide the join between basket and stems. Finish off the bottom edge of the basket in the same way.

3 Using the remaining dough make a collection of small cigar shapes for the flower heads, about 5cm (2in) long and lay these side by side in a row along the top of the stems.

4 The final step is not difficult but requires some patience. With your fingers, roll lots of tiny pieces of dough just like grains of rice. Place these on top of the cigar shapes to make up the lavender flower heads. Make sure they are positioned in such a way that they appear to be growing in an upwards direction, and ensure that the cigar shape is completely covered.

5 Push a large paper-clip into the centre top of the piece for hanging. Bake, paint as desired and varnish as instructed in Basic Techniques. Finally, for the finishing touch tie a few strands of natural raffia around the flower stems when the varnish is dry.

_T_his project is made from an ordinary quarry tile purchased from any DIY shop, which is decorated with gardening paraphernalia made from salt dough. The decoration is baked directly on to the tile, but you may find that it lifts off after baking, depending on how smooth the surface of the tile is. If this happens, the pieces can easily be glued back into place.

- *1 cup of flour made into dough (see page 11)*
- *A quarry tile with holes drilled in the top corners*
- *A piece of ribbon or string*
- *Knife*
- *Wooden skewer or cocktail stick*
- *Paint*
- *Varnish*
- *Glue (possibly!)*

1 Wet your quarry tile and work directly on to this. Construct the handles of the spade and fork from thin snakes of dough, tapered off to a point at the bottom end. At the top add a D-shaped grip as shown. Both the spade and the fork are oblong shapes cut from thinly rolled out dough with a slight V-shape indentation in the top for the handle to sit in. You will need to cut out three sections to make the tines of the fork.

2 For the watering can, cut an oblong of dough 3 x 5cm (1¼ x 2in) from dough rolled out to 1cm (½in) thick. With a skewer mark lines across the top and bottom. Add handles at the top and side made from snakes of dough. Finally mould the spout with a cone-shaped rose on top and attach to the side of the can, opposite the handle.

3 For the little potted plant, roll out a piece of dough to 1cm (½in) thick and cut a plant pot shape approximately 5cm (2in) deep and 2cm (¾in) wide at the base and 3.5cm (1½in) wide at the top. Cut a narrow strip of thinly rolled out dough and place this across the top for the rim of the pot. Fill the pot with a bundle of small leaves (see page 17).

4 Bake as instructed in Basic Techniques. If the models lift off the tile during baking simply glue them back into place once they are cold. Paint as desired and varnish according to the instructions in Basic Techniques. When dry, tie a piece of ribbon or string through the holes for hanging.

SUNFLOWERS & DAISIES

These flowers are charming and not difficult to make. They can be made as a model in their own right, planted in pots or used as a decoration on other items such as the little pictures or the letter rack and candle box in Part 7 (see page 108). The choice of colour for painting determines whether they are sunflowers or daisies.

- *2 cups flour made into dough (see page 11)*
- *Knife*
- *Wooden skewer or cocktail stick*
- *Medium paper-clip*
- *Paint*
- *Varnish*

1 Roll a snake of dough 1cm (½in) thick and about 20cm (8in) long for the stem. Place a flattened ball of dough 2.5cm (1in) diameter at the top, and another 7.5cm (3in) in diameter at the bottom, overlapping the circles of dough over the ends of the stem. Cut the large circle as shown to form the sides and base of the pot. The rounded top is left to give the effect of soil. Roll another snake of dough and flatten it. Place across the top of the pot to form the rim. Push a paper-clip into the ball of dough at the top for hanging – this will be hidden by the petals but after baking you will be able to thread a ribbon through it for hanging.

2 To make the petals, mould sixteen small pieces of dough to tiny cigar shapes. Flatten these with the palm of your hand and with the skewer mark a line up the centre of each. Place eight petals evenly around the edge of the flower head, and then the other eight in a second layer, filling the gaps between the original petals. Flatten another ball of dough to 2.5cm (1in) diameter and place in the centre of the flower covering the inside ends of the petals. Dot this with the blunt end of a skewer for texture.

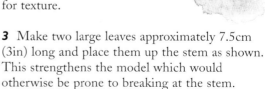

3 Make two large leaves approximately 7.5cm (3in) long and place them up the stem as shown. This strengthens the model which would otherwise be prone to breaking at the stem.

4 To make just the flower head flatten a ball of dough and then follow step 2. If this flower is to go in a picture, you will not need a paper-clip and you can make a larger number of finer petals as it will be protected by the picture frame.

5 Bake, paint as desired and varnish as instructed in Basic Techniques.

*T*he idea for this little plaque was adapted from a stencilled design on a lampshade. The gingham border and string hanger add a touch of the 'New England' look that is currently so popular.

- *3 cups flour made into dough (see page 11)*
- *A piece of nylon netting 15cm (6in) square*
- *Knife*
- *Wooden skewer*
- *Plastic drinking straw*
- *String*
- *70cm (¾yd) gingham ribbon 2.5cm (1in) wide*
- *PVA glue*
- *Paint*
- *Varnish*

1 Roll out your dough to an oblong at least 15 x 30cm (6 x 12in) and approximately 6mm (¼in) thick. Using the laminating technique (see page 11) fold over the dough and cut into a 15cm (6in) square. Lightly mark a 2.5cm (1in) border all round the edge with a knife, and using the plastic straw cut a hole in the centre top. The design is placed inside the border.

2 Roll a snake of dough for the tree trunk, flatten slightly and make cuts down from the top to divide it into branches (see page 17). Add a few extra trailing branches if required. Make a lot of small leaves and place them in clusters growing from the branches. Place several little apples amongst the leaves.

3 Make a small pot for the base of the tree by cutting a flowerpot shape from dough rolled out to approximately 6mm (¼in) thick, adding a rim across the top cut from thinly rolled out dough. Place a couple of fallen apples on the ground beside the tree and another resting on the pot.

4 Cut a small barrel from some thinly rolled out dough and mark vertical lines on it with a knife. Place a tiny flattened snake of dough around the barrel a little way down from the top and five tiny apples and a minute leaf on top of it.

5 Bake, paint as desired and varnish as instructed in Basic Techniques.

6 When the varnish is completely dry, glue the ribbon around the border, mitring the corners for a neat finish. Make a hole in the ribbon where there is a hole in the dough and thread the string through for a hanger.

This scarecrow is really fun to make and the raffia used for his hair and hands adds an authentic touch. If you prefer, you could dress him in some overalls rather than the traditional farmer's smock used here.

- *2 cups flour made into dough (see page 11)*
- *Knife*
- *Wooden skewer or cocktail stick*
- *Garlic press or potato ricer*
- *A few strands of raffia*
- *Medium paper-clip*
- *Paint*
- *Varnish*

1 Roll two snakes of dough approximately 2cm (³⁄₄in) thick and place in a cross shape, trimming to the required length for the arms and upright pole. Add a ball of dough at the top for the head, leaning slightly to the side.

2 Place a few strands of raffia at the ends of the arm poles, holding it in place by wetting the dough and sticking the raffia to it. Now make the smock. The body section is an oblong of thinly rolled dough laid over the upright pole and gathered into the neck area, smoothing the dough as you go. The sleeves are smaller oblongs cut from the same thinly rolled dough and wrapped around the arm poles. Try to join the sleeves to the body of the smock as neatly as possible and pinch the other end into a cuff, trapping the raffia. Mark the line of the cuff with a skewer, then mark the smocking over the chest with a knife.

3 Place some raffia on the head, holding it in place with water. Taking a semi-circle of thinly rolled out dough, mould a 'beanie' type hat and place on the head, trapping the raffia hair in place. Add button eyes and a carrot nose.

4 Place a snake of dough around the neck for a scarf, finishing it off with two long, thin, triangular tails cut from thinly rolled dough, and a small ball of dough over the join for the knot. Flatten a sausage of dough and place across the base of the upright pole, and cover this with grass extruded through a garlic press or potato ricer.

5 Push a paper-clip into the top of the head for hanging. Bake, paint and varnish as instructed in Basic Techniques.

There was obviously a very good crop of strawberries this year! The abundant fruits overflowing from this terracotta pot look good enough to eat. Because of the sheer number of them, you won't regret investing in some sugarcraft cutters for the leaves and blossom on this model.

- *3 cups flour made into dough (see page 11)*
- *Knife*
- *Wooden skewer or cocktail stick*
- *Sugarcraft cutters for leaves, blossom and strawberry stalks*
- *Tin foil*
- *Cloves*
- *Large paper-clip*
- *Paint*
- *Varnish*

1 Roll out half your dough to 1cm (⅜in) thick, and using the trace-off template on page 124, cut out the pot. Roll a snake of dough and lay across the top for the rim. Re-roll the trimmings and using the smaller templates cut the pockets to go on the sides and front of the pot. Shape these as required and attach to the pot, supporting them with scrunched-up pieces of tin foil so that they don't sink down.

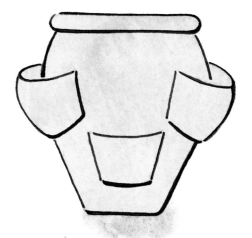

2 Thinly roll out some more of your dough and cut out lots and lots of leaves. If you have a sugarcraft cutter for this, the job will be quicker and the veins are already marked on. If you don't however, the bowl of a teaspoon with the handle bent back out of the way makes a good leaf-shaped cutter, and the veins can be marked with a skewer.

3 Next you need to make lots of strawberries. These are small cones of dough with a stalk added. Some of the strawberries can have stalks made from cloves with the seed head removed. For others, a star-shaped stalk can be cut from thinly rolled out dough with a sugarcraft cutter and joined to the strawberry by pushing a clove in head first. The spots for the strawberry seeds are best marked with a skewer after they are in place.

4 Arrange the leaves and strawberries in heaps growing out of the top and pockets of the pot. They do not have to be symmetrical and in fact look more natural if some clumps are larger than others. Dot over the strawberries with a skewer. Lastly, add several tiny flowers, either cut with a blossom cutter or moulded by hand (see page 17).

5 Push a large paper-clip into the top for hanging. Bake, paint and varnish as instructed in Basic Techniques.

The flowers growing on this simple little plaque are cut with a small heart-shaped cutter and a blossom cutter. If you don't have cutters it is easy to improvise and mould your own flowers. The unusual method of hanging this plaque gives it added interest.

- *1 cup flour made into dough (see page 11)*
- *Knife*
- *Wooden skewer or cocktail stick*
- *Small heart-shaped cutter and blossom cutter*
- *Plastic drinking straw*
- *Raffia or string*
- *Small stick*

1 Roll out your dough to approximately 1cm (³⁄₈in) thick, and cut a rectangle 15 x 12.5cm (6 x 5in). With the prongs of a fork, mark a ribbed effect all round the edge of the plaque. Cut holes in the top two corners using the straw.

3 To make the simple watering can, cut an oblong shape and the spout shape from rolled out dough and place on the plaque. Add a small rose, moulded by hand to the top of the spout, and a snake of dough bent round for the handle.

2 Re-roll the trimmings and cut out the window box to fit as shown. Roll a very thin snake of dough and cut off varying lengths for the flower stems. Place these at regular intervals growing out of the window box. Cut hearts and flowers from very thinly rolled dough and place alternately at the tops of the stems. Add several tiny little leaves moulded by hand with veins marked with a skewer (see page 17).

4 Bake, paint as desired and then varnish according to the instructions in Basic Techniques. When the varnish is completely dry, thread a few strands of raffia through the holes and tie into loops. Thread your stick through these loops and use it to hang the plaque on the wall.

This is another project where you really need an ivy leaf cutter to complete it in a reasonable time. If you don't have one, you could always make the model a different variety of houseplant, with larger leaves of a more simple shape.

- *2 cups flour made into dough (see page 11)*
- *Knife*
- *Ivy leaf cutter*
- *Large paper-clip*
- *Paint*
- *Varnish*

1 Roll out half your dough to 1cm (½in) thick and using the trace-off template on page 124 cut out the shape of the pot. Cut another strip of dough approximately 2.5cm (1in) wide and lay across the pot for the rim, in the position indicated by the dotted line on the template.

2 The rest of the project is simply a matter of rolling out the remainder of your dough quite thinly and cutting out what seems like hundreds of ivy leaves. When you have enough to make a start, begin arranging them on your plaque, starting with the area above the pot. Try to envisage the way they would grow naturally, which is likely to be cascading downwards, and do your best to achieve this effect.

3 For the trailing branches, obviously it is not possible to make them as thin and wispy as they would be on a real plant, as they would break straight off. It is therefore helpful to add some flattened snakes of dough cascading down from the main body of the plant and build up your layers of leaves on top of these for strength. When you are satisfied with the shape of your plant and are sure that it will be strong enough to withstand handling during painting and varnishing, push a large paper-clip into the top for hanging.

4 Bake as instructed in Basic Techniques and then paint. This project looks much more effective if you make the ivy leaves of the variegated variety. They are usually green and cream, so it is a good idea to leave the natural dough colour for the lighter parts. There are varieties of ivy with both cream centres and green edges or the reverse, so take your pick. Varnish according to the instructions in Basic Techniques.

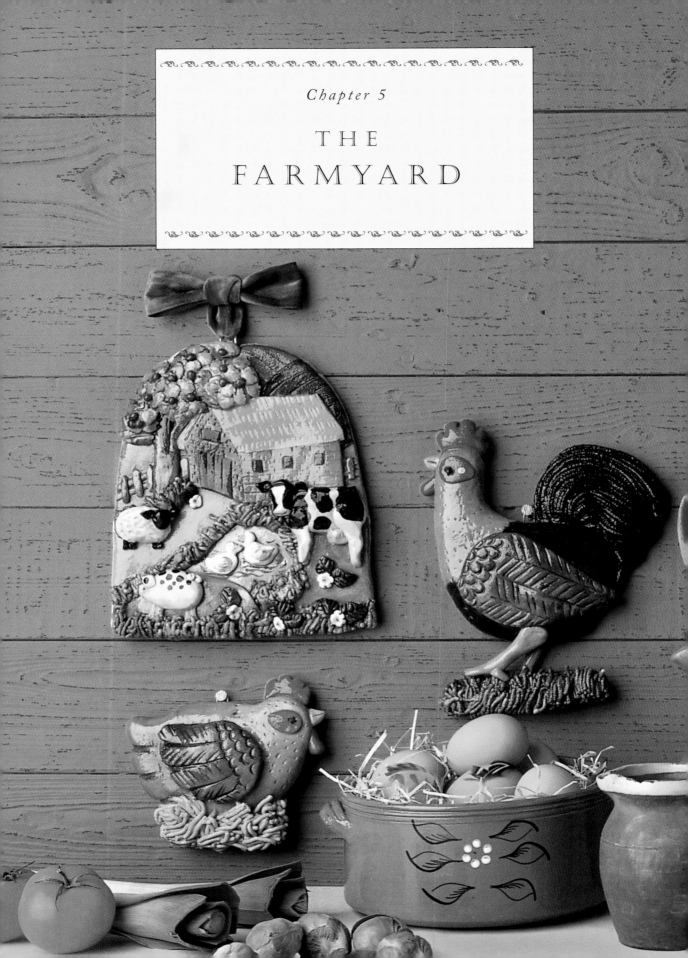

Chapter 5

THE
FARMYARD

This project features the idea of making decorated tiles from salt dough. The basic technique could be adapted to almost any design, for example decorating with flowers or perhaps illustrating hobbies or sports.

- *2 cups flour made into dough (see page 11)*
- *Sharp knife*
- *Wooden skewer or cocktail stick*
- *Cloves*
- *Large plastic drinking straw*
- *String*
- *Fork*
- *Ruler*

1 Roll out half your dough to 1cm (³⁄₈in) thick. With a sharp knife, and using the edge of a ruler to cut against, cut a 15cm (6in) square. Using the prongs of a fork mark all around the outer edge of the tile as shown. From the rolled out dough also cut a triangle for the roof with a base 17.5cm (7in) wide. Using the plastic drinking straw as a cutter, make holes in the top corners of the tile, and in all three corners of the roof. With a knife mark horizontal lines across the roof.

2 Roll out a fat sausage of dough and flatten it to form the cow's body. Pinch the top right-hand corner to a point for the hip bone then lay the body on the tile.

3 Using the first two fingers of one hand and working against the palm of the other hand, roll out a thin piece of dough for each of the cow's legs. Where your two fingers come together, the dough will naturally form a lump for the knee joint. Slip the first two legs under the body, add an udder, and the attach the remaining two legs to

the top of the body. Roll a snake of dough for the tail, wider at the bottom, and attach, marking the hairs at the end with a knife.

4 Make an inverted pear shape for the head and attach to the body. Add pointed ears sticking out at right angles to the head, and a small piece of dough for the top knot. Mark the nostrils with a skewer and add cloves for eyes.

5 The milk pail is cut from a piece of dough rolled out to 6mm (¹⁄₄in) thick with a very thin snake of dough for the handle. The milking stool has three small sausages of dough for the legs (the middle one being slightly shorter), and a rather fatter sausage squashed flat for the seat. See diagram opposite. These are placed in position on the tile, which is now ready for baking.

6 Take extra care when baking flat items such as the tile and roof as they are liable to rise and

bubble. The best way to avoid this is to start off the cooking process at no more than 100°C (200°F/Gas Mark ¼). The temperature can be raised to 120°C (230°F/Gas Mark ½) after a few hours once the pieces have started to harden.

7 Paint as desired and varnish according to the instructions in Basic Techniques. When the varnish is dry, use string threaded through the holes to attach the tile to the roof, and to make a hanger for the tile.

*T*his broody hen and proud cockerel would be an asset to any country house. They are bright and colourful and would look delightful hung on a kitchen wall.

- *4 cups flour made into dough (see page 11)*
- *Wooden skewer or cocktail stick*
- *Potato ricer or garlic press*
- *Cloves*
- *2 large paper-clips*
- *Paint*
- *Varnish*

1 For the hen, take an orange-sized ball of dough and flatten and shape it as shown in the diagram. Using the skewer, draw up the tail area and make three indentations as shown.

2 For the wing, flatten a pear-shaped piece of dough and draw up the edges in the same way as with the body. Mark three rows of feathers using the end of a paper-clip and then mark the rest of the wing with a knife as shown.

3 Small balls of dough are shaped and added for the facial detail including the beak. A clove is pushed in for the eye. The straw nest is made by piling up a quantity of extruded dough beneath the body (see page 18).

4 For the cockerel, take a ball of dough the size of a large orange and flatten and shape as shown in the diagram. Add the wing in the same way as for the hen but without drawing up the edge. The facial detail is also added in the same way as the hen but the comb on top of the head is larger.

5 For the tail feathers you can either use dough extruded through a potato ricer (as in the photograph) if you have one with large enough holes in it, or otherwise roll out lots of thin snakes of dough and pile them up on top of each other. When adding the tail, bear in mind that for the cockerel to hang straight on the wall, the tail must balance against the head.

6 Referring to diagram opposite, roll a sausage of dough for the back leg, about 5cm (2in) long and tuck underneath the body. Roll another sausage of dough to act as a base for the grass and place across the bottom, slightly overlapping the bottom of the back leg. Lay grass made from extruded dough on top of this. Finally, roll another sausage for the top leg, flattening it slightly as you attach it to the body. Flatten the other end of the leg for the foot and snip the claws with a small pair of scissors. Add the back claw made from a tiny piece of dough. This top leg will need to be supported during baking on a scrunched-up piece of tin foil to stop it sagging. Mark the breast feathers on both the hen and cockerel by dotting with a stick.

7 Push the large paper-clips into the tops of your models and then bake, paint as desired and varnish according to the instructions in Basic Techniques.

PAIR OF GEESE

These delightfully old-fashioned looking geese have been given their antique look by varnishing in a slightly different way from usual. The female sits on her nest while the male stands protectively over her. Both wear matching gingham neck ribbons.

- *4 cups of flour made into dough (see page 11)*
- *Wooden skewer or cocktail stick*
- *Knife*
- *2 large paper-clips*
- *Cloves*
- *Ribbon*
- *Paint*
- *Varnish*

1 The bodies of both the geese are made in the same way, each from a ball of dough the size of a large orange, as shown in the diagram. They face in opposite directions and the head of the female is bent over to give the impression of looking behind her. Using a wooden stick, mark a ridge to give the shape of the head.

2 The wings are made in exactly the same way as instructed for the cockerel (see page 74), marking the feathers with a paper-clip and a knife. The beak is a cone-shaped piece of dough attached to the head with a little water and the opening marked with a knife. A nostril is marked on the beak with a skewer, and cloves pushed in for eyes.

3 For the male, two feet are made from sausages of dough flattened out into triangular webbed feet at the ends and slipped under the body. The webbing on the feet is marked with a skewer (see below left).

4 For the female, a sausage of dough is flattened and curled around the bottom of the body as a base to build the nest on. The nest is made with five leaves (see page 17) laying these over the top of the sausage, touching the body.

5 Push a large paper-clip into the top of each goose for hanging. Bake, paint as desired and varnish as instructed in Basic Techniques, or in the following way if you prefer an antique look.

Paint the models, using white for the bodies. When the paint is dry, rub all over with a soft cloth dipped in satin-finish coloured varnish. The one used here has a teak stain in it. Use an oil-based varnish and not a quick-drying acrylic one as these will take off the paint. Finally, give the geese two coats of satin-finish polyurethane wood varnish. When dry tie a ribbon around their necks.

*T*his project takes the idea of using dough tiles as in the cowshed (see page 72) a stage further, by stringing three together. You could adapt the same idea for use with other animals such as a pig sty or a sheep pen, by making two or three tiles and hanging them together either vertically or horizontally.

- *2 cups of flour made into dough (see page 11)*
- *Sharp knife*
- *Wooden skewer or cocktail stick*
- *Large plastic straw*
- *Potato ricer or garlic press*
- *Fork*
- *String*
- *Paint*
- *Varnish*

1 Following the instructions for the cowshed (see page 72) make three tiles each 10cm (4in) square. Mark the edges with a fork and using the plastic straw cut holes in all four corners of two of the tiles and in just the top two corners of the third. From the rolled out dough cut a triangular roof with a base 12.5cm (5in) wide. Mark the edges with a fork and cut holes in all three corners with the plastic straw.

2 Following the instructions for the hen (see page 74), make two small hens facing in opposite directions and lay them onto what will be the top and bottom tiles, ie, one tile with four holes, and the bottom tile with two holes. Lay a straw nest beneath one of these hens as on page 74, and model legs and feet for the other from very thin snakes of dough.

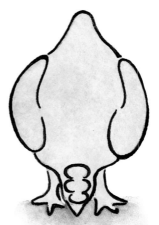

3 For the centre hen which is pecking at corn, model the body as though it is being viewed from above, and tuck two small feet made from very thin snakes of dough under either side of the head.

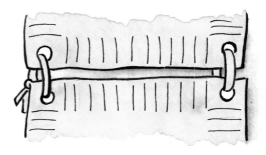

4 Bake the tiles, taking care to start off the baking process slowly as detailed on page 73. Paint as desired and varnish according to the instructions in Basic Techniques. When dry, string the tiles together as shown and add a loop of string through the top of the roof for hanging.

These little rabbits would look lovely on a nursery wall, framed as in the photograph. For a more natural look, try making them individually and painting them brown or grey to look like little wild rabbits.

- 2 cups flour made into dough (see page 11)
- Wooden skewer or cocktail stick
- Knife
- 4 black-headed map pins
- Picture frame 38 x 12.5cm (15 x 5in) without glass
- Piece of coloured card or mountboard to fit frame
- Self-adhesive sticky pads
- Paint
- Varnish

1 Take a small amount of your dough and roll out to 6mm (¼in) thick. Using the trace-off template on page 125 cut a small heart shape for the centre of the picture.

2 The rabbits are made from a number of different sized, pear-shaped pieces of dough joined together. You will need to make two rabbits, exactly the same but facing in opposite directions. First take a ball of dough about the size of plum, mould it into a pear shape and flatten slightly for the body. Take another ball of dough about half the size of the first and mould this also into a pear shape only not quite so elongated as the body. This piece forms the head, and should be attached to the thin end of the body as shown.

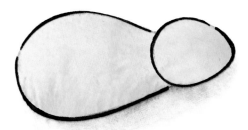

3 The legs are made from two more pear-shaped pieces, the back leg being slightly larger than the front. Mould the legs slightly thinner at the ends

and bend round for the feet. Attach to the body at either end as shown. Add two ears moulded from flattened cigar shapes, and a small ball of dough for the tail.

4 Mark the whiskers with a knife and push black-headed map pins into your models for eyes and noses. If you don't have map pins, cloves will do. Lastly roughen up the texture of the tail with a skewer to make it look fluffy.

5 Bake, paint as desired and varnish according to the instructions in Basic Techniques. When the varnish is dry you can attach your models to the piece of card or mountboard using plenty of self-adhesive sticky pads, and then mount in the frame.

These sheep jumping over a five-bar gate would make an amusing decoration for an insomniac's bedroom! They are very simple to make and of course could be displayed individually or made as a pair of ewe and ram facing in opposite directions.

- *3 cups flour made into dough (see page 11)*
- *Wooden skewer or cocktail stick*
- *Knife*
- *Cloves*
- *Large paper-clips*
- *Paint*
- *Varnish*

1 To make the gate, roll out a snake of dough about 1cm (³⁄₈in) diameter and flatten it. Cut into approximately 15cm (6in) lengths and construct the gate as shown, laying a longer bar diagonally across the other five. Trim the ends level and add two slightly thicker flattened snakes of dough for the upright posts. If you have difficulty in getting the perspective right, trace the template on page 125 onto baking parchment and model your gate directly on to this.

2 For each sheep's body (see below left), take a ball of dough the size of an orange, roll into a fat sausage shape and flatten slightly. Roll a long snake of dough for the legs and cut two 15cm (6in) lengths. Fold these in half and tuck well under the body as shown. Mark the hooves with a knife.

3 Place an oval-shaped piece of dough in position for the head, altering the position with each sheep slightly to add variety. For the ram, make two horns by rolling snakes of dough and attaching to the head as shown. Add long, pointed ears, bearing in mind that sheeps' ears grow out of the side of their heads, not straight up on top.

4 Push in cloves for eyes and mark nose and mouth with a stick. Roughen up the wool by marking with the blunt end of a wooden skewer. Push a large paper-clip into the top of each sheep for hanging. You do not need to put one in the gate as the bars will act as a hanger.

5 Bake, paint as desired and varnish according to the instruction in Basic Techniques. When dry hang on the wall in a line, placing the sheep as if queuing up to jump over the gate!

This project utilises the amazing capacity salt dough has of moulding itself to a piece of wood during baking. The design was inspired by the many naive paintings of farm animals that are so popular nowadays. The antique effect was created in the same way as with the geese on page 76.

- *2 cups flour made into dough (see page 11)*
- *A piece of natural, untreated wood approximately 38 x 12.5cm (15 x 5in)*
- *Wooden skewer or cocktail stick*
- *Potato ricer or garlic press*
- *Paint*
- *Varnish*
- *String*

1 Brush your piece of wood with water, making sure that it is well moistened all over. Take two balls of dough about the size of apples and mould into pear shapes. Making sure that they are facing in opposite directions, flatten and attach to the wood. Using a blunt instrument such as the flat end of a pencil, squash the snouts flat and mark nostrils with a skewer.

2 Roll a long snake of dough for the legs and cut two 15cm (6in) lengths for each pig. Fold in half and tuck under the body as for the sheep in the previous project. Mark the trotters with a knife.

3 Mould four tiny pear-shaped pieces of dough for the ears and attach two to each pig, one tucked under the head as shown and the other on the top. Roll a very thin snake of dough and attach to the bottom of each pig, twisting as you do so to form a curly tail.

4 Mark eyes and mouths with a skewer and place a strip of extruded dough for grass (see page 18) along the bottom edge of the wood.

5 Bake, paint as desired and varnish as instructed in Basic Techniques, or as described on page 76 if you prefer an antique finish. On the model in the photograph, the coloured effect on the wood is achieved by brushing over with a very thin wash of blue/green water colour paint.

6 When completely dry, drill a hole in each of the upper corners and thread through some string for hanging, tying knots on the front to hold the string in place.

This farm scene although appearing complicated is really just a collection of several of the previous simpler projects grouped together.

- *4 cups flour made into dough (see page 11)*
- *Knife*
- *A piece of nylon netting about 30cm (12in) square*
- *Wooden skewer or cocktail stick*
- *Potato ricer or garlic press*
- *Very large paper-clip*

1 Following the instructions for laminating in Basic Techniques (see page 11) and, using the trace-off basic plaque template on page 125, create the wall plaque from about half your dough.

2 Roll out a piece of dough to 6mm (¼in) thick and using the template on page 125, cut out the barn and lay in position on your plaque. With a knife or skewer mark the windows, door, brickwork and thatch on the barn.

3 Roll a thin snake of dough, flatten and cut into lengths to make the fence on either side of the barn as shown. Following the instructions in Basic Techniques (see page 17), make a tree and place to the left of the barn with the leaves growing over the roof.

4 Flatten a sausage of dough to make the small hillock in the bottom left-hand corner of the plaque. With short lengths of extruded dough (see page 18) mark out the area for the path and the pond and place a strip along the bottom edge of the plaque.

5 The pig, sheep and cow are made in exactly the same way as instructed in the previous projects in this chapter but on a smaller scale (see pages 84, 82 and 72). Once made, they are positioned on the plaque.

6 The tiny ducks are moulded from very small pear-shaped pieces of dough with a little ball for the head and a tiny cone for the beak, marked with a knife. The wings are painted on.

7 Finally, mark the ploughed fields in the top right-hand corner with a knife and scatter a few leaves and flowers around (see page 17).

8 Push a very large paper-clip into the top of the plaque for hanging. Bake, paint as desired and varnish as instructed in Basic Techniques.

Chapter 6

COUNTRY LIFE

An old-fashioned milk stand with a slab on top for standing the churns on ready for collection can be seen at the end of many farm driveways. This plaque is quite simple to make, and the honey-coloured Cotswold stone wall makes it particularly attractive. You could add a few flowers for a little more colour.

- *2 cups flour made into dough (see page 11)*
- *Knife*
- *Wooden skewer or cocktail stick*
- *Potato ricer or garlic press*
- *Medium paper-clip*
- *Paint (including silver)*
- *Varnish*

1 Roll out half your dough with a rolling pin to approximately 8mm (³⁄₈in) thick and with a knife cut to an irregular shape for the background. With your hands, mould an oblong shape approximately 5 x 7.5cm (2 x 3in) and 1cm (¹⁄₂in) thick, and place this centrally towards the bottom of the plaque for the base of the stand.

2 For the stone effect, break off small pieces of dough and flatten them between your fingers to small oblong shapes. Lay these first over the milk stand as though building up a wall. When the stand is covered, cut a strip from dough rolled out to 6mm (¹⁄₄in) thick and place this across the top of the stand for the slab that the churns rest on.

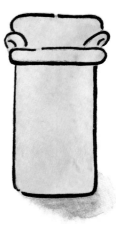

3 Next make the churns. These are made from sausages of dough, flattened slightly and trimmed to shape, with a smaller, flattened sausage laid across the top for the lid. Thin snakes of dough are used for the rim and handles, but these are added at the end. Stand the churns on the milk stand.

4 Now cover the background wall with stones in the same way as you built up the wall effect on the stand, leaving a gap at the side for the bush. Make sure that the stones butt neatly up to the edge of the churns. Lay the stone pieces vertically in a row along the top of the wall and, with the blunt end of a skewer, prod at the wall to produce the uneven effect of stone.

5 Make a bush at the side by building up pieces of pinched dough (see page 17), and finish off with a row of grass extruded through a garlic press or potato ricer across the bottom (see page 18). Finally, add thin snakes of dough for the rims and handles of the churns.

6 Push a paper-clip into the top for hanging and bake, paint and varnish as instructed in Basic Techniques.

*T*his plaque was inspired by a beautiful ceramic piece hanging on a friend's wall. Old Land Rovers like this one are firm favourites with farmers and can often be seen in various states of disrepair, in tumbledown barns or farmyards.

- *4 cups flour made into dough (see page 11)*
- *Piece of nylon netting 15 x 20cm (6 x 8in)*
- *Knife*
- *Wooden skewer or cocktail stick*
- *Very large paper-clip*
- *Garlic press or potato ricer*
- *Paint*
- *Varnish*

1 Using the laminating technique (see page 11) and the trace-off basic plaque template on page 125, follow the instructions in Basic Techniques to create the wall plaque.

2 With a knife, roughly mark the shape and position of the vehicle on your plaque – this will give you a guideline to work to. Roll some thin snakes of dough, flatten them and place in position for the windscreen and steering wheel. Add a flattened sausage for the roof, and a thin strip of rolled out dough just below the windscreen as shown.

You will need to flatten the bonnet piece and the tops of the wings towards the back, so that they fit neatly up against the base of the windscreen.

4 Mark the radiator grille with a knife, and using small pieces of dough add the various lights, badges and number plate. A flattened sausage is placed on the bonnet for the spare tyre, and two smaller ones for the front tyres. Mark the tread on these with a knife. Finally, add a long snake of dough for the bumper, flattened and wrapped around the front of the car.

5 Add a tree up either side of the plaque (see page 17) and grass extruded from a potato ricer or garlic press across the bottom and round the base of the trees (see page 18).

3 Next build up the front of the car from pieces cut from dough rolled out to approximately 1cm (³⁄₈in) thick. Follow the guidelines marked on the plaque for size, and cut the shapes as shown in the diagram, fitting them together like a jigsaw puzzle.

6 Push a very large paper-clip into the top for hanging, and bake, paint and varnish as instructed in Basic Techniques.

This small plaque is simple to make but effective. You could adapt it to suit your home, perhaps by adding a coloured rug on the hearth or making the fire surround in a brick or stone effect rather than wood. In this case, the wood effect was achieved by rubbing a stained varnish into the dough.

- *3 cups flour made into dough (see page 11)*
- *Knife*
- *Wooden skewer or cocktail stick*
- *Black-headed map pin for cat's nose*
- *2 medium paper-clips*
- *Paint*
- *Varnish*

1 Roll out half your dough to 6mm (¼in) thick and using the trace-off template on page 126, cut out the shape of the fireplace. With a knife, gently mark in the border where the wooden surround will go. From thinly rolled out dough, using the inner part of the template, cut out the black cast iron plate and position on the plaque. Mark the inside edge of the arched part with a fork for a decorative effect.

2 Now cut some strips of dough rolled out to 6mm (¼in) thick for the wooden surround and for the hearth, and lay these in position on the plaque, attaching them with a little water. Mark the tiles of the hearth and the beaded edges of the surround with a knife. Add a flattened sausage of dough across the top for the mantelpiece, and little decorative brackets moulded by hand. If you wish you can mark a woodgrain on these with a knife.

3 Mould the fire basket to fit into the base of the archway and cut small chunks of dough for the coals. Mark lines across the front of the fire basket with a knife and add a small knob in the centre.

4 Finally, make a small cat curled up in front of the fire. He is moulded from balls of dough put together as shown, with little pointed ears and a long tail wrapped round his body. The cheeks are little flattened balls of dough with whiskers marked with a cocktail stick and a black-headed map pin pushed in for his nose. If you don't have one, simply add a tiny ball of dough.

5 If you wish you could add some decorative pieces sitting on top of the mantelpiece – why not take some ideas from the dresser project on page 46?

6 Push the paper-clips in at either side on top of the mantelpiece and bake, paint as desired and varnish as instructed in Basic Techniques.

This rather amusing little chap was adapted from a cast iron doorstop and would make a great gift for a golfing companion. You could also quite easily change the features and clothes to make a lady golfer.

- *3 cups flour made into dough (see page 11)*
- *Knife*
- *Wooden skewer or cocktail stick*
- *Garlic press or potato ricer*
- *Small paper-clip*
- *Paint*
- *Varnish*

)1 Mould the basic figure as instructed on page 19. As you create the legs, make them in two parts to give the effect of plus fours. The arms are also made wide enough for the sleeves of the jacket, and so are better added after you have clothed the body.

2 Once you have moulded the head, torso, legs and feet add the jacket details. The collar and tie are cut from very thinly rolled out dough with a sharp knife and placed in position at the neck. The body of the coat is cut from very thinly rolled out dough as shown, to fit around the torso and laid over the body. The revers of the jacket are cut separately and laid on top.

3 Now make the golf bag from a long sausage of dough cut off at the ends. The little clubs are moulded by hand and placed at the top end of the bag, and thin snakes of dough are added for the strap detail. Lay the golf bag in position across the body and add the arms and hands wrapped around the bag in a carrying position.

4 For the facial detail, add a nose and ears as instructed on page 19 and mould a nice bushy moustache to place under the nose. The mouth and eyes are painted on after baking. Mould a peaked cap in two pieces, and sit it on top of the head, with a tiny piece of dough added at each side for the hair. Texture can be marked in this with a knife.

5 Finally, stand your chap on a flattened sausage of dough covered with extruded grass (see page 18)

6 Push a paper-clip into his head for hanging and bake, paint as desired and varnish as instructed in Basic Techniques.

I couldn't resist including these wonderfully amusing figures designed by my friend Louise Dalby, and my thanks to her for allowing me to do so. The technique involved in producing these bathing beauties requires a certain amount of sculpting skill but don't let this deter you, as by studying the photograph carefully you will be able to copy the details without difficulty. Louise brings real life to her figures by making them in such interesting positions rather than standing stiffly. This takes some imagination and a little practice but is definitely worth persevering with.

- *2 cups flour made into dough (see page 11)*
- *Knife*
- *Modelling tool such as round-bladed knife*
- *Wooden skewer or cocktail stick*
- *Garlic press*
- *Small paper-clip*

1 Depending on which figure you are making, the details will vary so study the photograph for the exact requirements, but there are certain principles common to all. Mould the head, torso, legs and arms as shown on page 19, but altering the shape to suit the figure you are making. In these cases the figures are notably fatter.

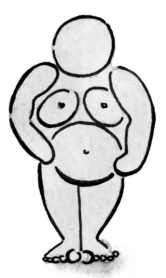

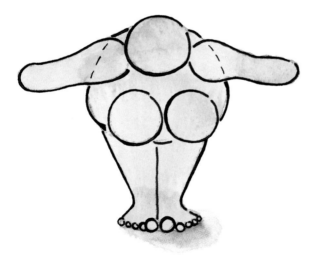

2 When assembling the component parts of the body, mould them together so that the joins don't show, by using a round-bladed knife dipped in water to smooth over the joins. Position the arms and legs as required, and then add over-large feet with tiny balls of dough stuck on for the toes. Smooth over the joins as before.

3 Next you need to sculpt the body shape. In the case of the women this means adding enormous breasts, and with the men, a pot-belly, and shaping the chest muscles slightly before adding tiny flattened balls of dough for the nipples. You will find that the dough can quite easily be shaped with a wet knife or modelling tool.

4 Add the swimsuit (or towel) cut from very thinly rolled out dough and laid in place over the body. Finally, add hair, made with a garlic press, and a nose and ears if required. The other facial details are painted on after baking.

5 Push a paper-clip into the head for hanging and bake, paint as desired and varnish as instructed in Basic Techniques.

This model is a little different from the others and would appeal to anybody who has needlecraft as a hobby. A little bit of sewing is involved in the making of this piece, so you will need to know how to do blanket stitch or buttonhole stitch.

- *2 cups flour made into dough (see page 11)*
- *Knife*
- *Button thread*
- *Embroidery silk*
- *Large plastic drinking straw*
- *Tapestry needle*
- *String for hanging*
- *Glue*
- *Paint*
- *Varnish*

1 Roll out you dough to 1cm (³⁄₈in) thick and using the trace-off template on page 126 cut out the heart shape. Using the plastic straw, cut a hole in the centre top, and then with the skewer poke holes at regular intervals all the way around the edge for stitching through. It is important to make sure that each hole goes right through and is big enough so that it doesn't close up again on baking.

2 Re-roll the trimmings and following the instructions in the quilt picture project (see page 30), make a few small buttons. Cut an oblong shape from the rolled-out dough for the cotton reel, adding a strip along the top and bottom to give it the right shape. Lastly, mould the thimble shape, marking dots in the top part of it with a skewer or cocktail stick and adding a very thin snake of dough for the rim.

3 Bake all these parts separately on your tray, as described in Basic Techniques, and when cooked paint as desired. The pewter effect of the thimble was achieved with a thin coat of silver over black.

4 Using coloured embroidery silk, sew all round the edge of the heart in blanket stitch, threading your needle through the holes as you go. Varnish all the pieces as instructed in Basic Techniques.

5 Assemble your model by wrapping thread around the cotton reel and threading the needle through it. Thread a short length of button thread through each button and tie off. Arrange the cotton reel, thimble and buttons on the heart, and when satisfied with their positions glue into place. Thread string or ribbon through the top of the heart for hanging.

FISHING TROPHY

This is 'one I caught earlier'! Salt dough is an ideal medium for a project like this and the results are extremely realistic. It is a good idea to find a picture of the fish you want to make and copy it as accurately as possible. Failing that, study the photograph opposite and work from that. The scales are made using nylon netting and the realistic effect is achieved by careful use of paints, using silver for the shimmer on the scales. I used the lid of an old cigar box for the case, but if you don't have anything similar you could simply mount your fish on a piece of wood. This could be framed later, or just drilled for hanging with string as in the kissing pigs project (see page 84).

- *2 cups flour made into dough (see page 11)*
- *Knife*
- *Wooden skewer or cocktail stick*
- *A piece of nylon netting*
- *Wood or box for mounting*
- *String for hanging*
- *Paint (including silver)*
- *Satin-finish varnish*

1 Wet your box or piece of wood and work directly on to it. With your hands, mould the torpedo shape of the trout's body and place on the wood. Add a tail cut from flattened dough and, using a wet knife, mould the tail to the body so that the join doesn't show. Mark the lines on the tail with a sharp knife. Mark the mouth and gills with a skewer.

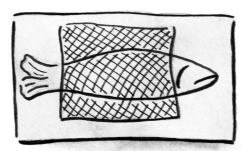

2 The effect of the scales is achieved at this stage by pressing a piece of nylon netting into the body of the fish, trying to make sure that it is applied with even pressure all over. The netting is then lifted off to reveal a textured surface. The full effect of this will only be seen after painting. Make sure that you only texture the area behind the gills as fish don't have scales on their faces.

3 Add an eye made from two flattened balls of dough, a smaller one placed on top of a slightly larger one. The various fins are shaped from small pieces of dough, flattened and marked with a knife. They are then attached to the body in the relevant positions.

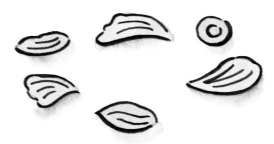

4 Bake as instructed in Basic Techniques and then paint. I used a combination of grey, brown, pink and black, all watered down very thinly and just washed over the dough. When this was dry I brushed a thin layer of silver paint over the whole fish, using an almost dry brush so that the silver just highlighted the raised areas. The eye is picked out in silver with a black centre. The box was painted with the same gouache paints as the doughcraft, the background being given a very thin wash of greenish-blue, and the frame picked out with a thicker coat of dark green.

5 When the paint is dry, varnish with satin-finish varnish and drill two holes in the wood to thread the string through for hanging.

*T*his chap, relaxing at the end of the day with his toe poking out of his sock, is probably the most complicated project in the book, so practice on some of the more simple designs before this one. A friend had a similar plaque made for her husband's fortieth birthday, but as he was in the motor trade, the paraphernalia surrounding the figure was relevant to that, and the doll made to look like him, so this figure can be adapted to suit another occupation or hobby.

● *3 cups flour made into dough (see page 11)*
● *Knife*
● *Wooden skewer or cocktail stick*
● *Garlic press*
● *Pencil*
● *Black-headed map pin*
● *2 paper-clips*

1 Begin by modelling the chair. All the pieces are moulded by hand and then fitted together. Start with a thickish oblong of dough for the seat and place another, slightly thinner above it for the back. Now add two sausages of dough at the sides for the arms of the chair, and a large, flattened, curved sausage for the floor and rug, placed below the chair. Two small balls of dough are used for the feet of the chair.

2 Make the legs from two sausages of dough rolled thickly enough to allow for trousers, and place these in a crossed position on the chair seat. Add the torso and head, leaning them against the chair back. Add the sweater cut from a piece of very thinly rolled out dough and lay over the body. The arms are still not in place at this point (see diagram above right). Add a polo neck to the sweater by placing a flattened sausage of dough around the neck.

3 The arms are added next, rolled thickly enough to allow for the sleeves of the sweater. Join the arms to the body and position as shown in the photograph. Mark the knitting on the sweater with a sharp knife. Cut the book from a piece of rolled out dough, marking the spine and pages with a knife, and placing it to lean against the body. This will probably need to be supported during baking with a ball of scrunched-up tin foil. Make a little coffee mug to sit on the arm of the chair (this again will probably need supporting with tin foil) and then add the two hands, one holding the coffee cup and the other the book. Add feet at the bottom of the trouser legs, with a tiny ball of dough for the protruding toe!

4 Mark the edge of the rug with a knife, and place the two magazines, cut from very thinly rolled out dough on the floor. Make a pair of wellington boots as instructed in the cooking range project (see page 50) and place by the arm of the chair.

5 The bearded collie lying by the side of the chair is the easiest type of dog to make as it is simply a mass of hair! You only need to make the head of the dog, resting on two paws made from small balls of dough with the claws marked with a skewer. Construct the head from balls and sausages of dough as shown in the diagram, and cover with long hair extruded from a garlic press and arranged with a centre parting! Push a black-headed map pin in for the nose, and make a little pink tongue to hang out of his mouth.

6 Finally, add facial detail as required – in this case eyes, nose, ears, bushy eyebrows and wavy hair. The mouth is painted on after baking. The head may need supporting with a scrunched-up piece of tin foil during baking to stop it falling off the back of the chair!

7 Mark the buttoning on the chair by pushing the point of a pencil through a plastic bag into the dough. Push paper-clips into the back of the chair on each side, and bake, paint and varnish as instructed in Basic Techniques.

Chapter 7

DECORATING WITH DOUGH

DECORATING WITH DOUGH

This section of the book deals with the concept of using salt dough to decorate items made from other materials, taking the craft of salt dough sculpture into another dimension. Obviously some materials are better suited to this technique than others but almost anything can be decorated from everyday household items to unfinished items made from wood or medium-density fibreboard (MDF).

ADDING DOUGHCRAFT DECORATIONS

In some cases it is necessary to make your doughcraft decoration in the traditional way and then use PVA glue to attach it to the piece you are decorating. This method is, however, not ideal for a number of reasons. First, it means that the item you are decorating must have a completely flat surface as the dough will be baked on a flat baking tray. Theoretically this means the dough should have a completely flat back but sometimes it distorts slightly during baking which means it may not lie flush against the piece you are decorating. Second, when gluing well-varnished dough onto another item, it is quite difficult to get the dough to adhere well because the varnish is so smooth and shiny. Much better results can be achieved with this method if it is possible to glue the decoration in place *before* varnishing and then varnish the entire piece well after painting.

The alternative method for attaching the dough decorations is to bake them in place. This obviously puts certain constraints on your work, mainly that the piece you are decorating must be able to fit in the oven, which could be a problem, for example, with a piece of furniture! Incidentally, furniture looks wonderful decorated with salt dough, and it really is amazingly tough. In this case it will obviously be necessary for you to bake your decoration separately.

ITEMS SUITABLE FOR DOUGHCRAFT DECORATION

Because of the low temperatures involved in baking doughcraft, almost any material will withstand the heat of the oven. Porous substances work best, such as unvarnished wood, medium density fibreboard (MDF), and even paper or papier-mâché. In the case of these materials, if you wet the surface slightly and then assemble the dough decoration directly on to the surface, when the whole thing is baked in the oven the dough will be stuck like concrete to the piece and will stay in place far more firmly than if it were glued on. Some metals also appear to exhibit this property, although I haven't been able to do enough research to determine exactly which ones. It seems to be that if the surface of the metal is slightly rough the dough will stick better than on a shiny, polished surface.

When dealing with non-porous items such as glass, ceramics, plastics, some metals and varnished wood, it is still a good idea to bake your dough directly on to the item you are decorating, as it will mould itself perfectly to the shape during baking, and even though it will lift off once cooked it can quickly be glued into place, preferably before varnishing, as already mentioned.

Using salt dough as a decorative medium means that you can combine the three-dimensional effect of dough sculpture with the most up-to-the-minute paint effects such as sponging, rag rolling, stencilling and colour washing. It is advisable to paint your piece before decorating with dough and baking, as it is particularly difficult to paint neatly around the edges of the decoration, especially if using any of the paint effects mentioned. The low temperatures used will not cause the paint to discolour. I should warn you, however, that if you paint the item completely, you will lose the adhering property of the dough on porous materials, and not only will the decoration come off, but it will bring the paint with it. The answer to this problem is to roughly draw the shape of your decoration in the correct position and then paint round it, leaving that area free of paint. It doesn't matter that the painted surface extends slightly under the dough decoration as long as there is a large enough area left blank to hold the dough in place. Having done this, dampen the area you have left blank, and assemble the dough directly onto your piece.

Many crafts that are popular today, such as découpage and folk art, make use of the idea of decorating a useful item rather than simply creating a picture. To this end a number of companies have sprung up in recent years supplying unpainted pieces especially for decorating yourself. These tend to be made from wood, papier-mâché or MDF (medium density fibreboard) and are all ideal for decorating with salt dough. A huge range of items

are available, from the little wooden yo-yos and boxes on page 110, through firescreens and clocks to furniture such as chests and dressers. Smaller items are widely available from craft shops, but you will probably need to visit a hobbyist exhibition or contact a manufacturer direct for larger items.

Most of the pieces shown in this chapter came from Blankers, a mail order company in Honiton, Devon, England (Telephone 01404 881667). One source for unfinished wood items in the United States is K. C.'s Wood Products, Freeport, Maine (207 865 3244). Small items can be obtained from any store that has tole painting equipment. Of course the idea of decorating with dough is also a brilliant way of 'doing up' an old piece that you may well have otherwise relegated to the dustbin!

PAINTING DOUGHCRAFT

When painting items to be decorated with dough you can use a number of different types of paint. The best are water-based paints, particularly if the painted item is going into the oven; a gloss or other oil-based paint will discolour and smell awful! If you need the durability associated with paints such as these, this can easily be achieved by applying two or three coats of varnish on top of the paint. If you are painting a wooden piece you can use a thin wash of ordinary water colour or gouache paint which will let the grain of the wood show through, or alternatively, emulsion for a more solid finish. MDF pieces need to be painted with emulsion as the fibreboard does not have an

attractive finish so needs to be well covered. There are many emulsion paints on the market today which will cover in one coat, and they are available in a wide range of colours. The little tester pots which can be bought very cheaply are ideal for small projects.

The gallery of photographs on the following pages will give you just a small idea of some of the things that you can do with salt dough and hopefully will inspire you to start hunting for something to decorate. Most of the designs I have used are taken from or adapted from the other projects in this book, but don't be afraid to 'do your own thing'!

BOXES & YO-YOS

These little balsa wood boxes can be purchased very cheaply from art and craft suppliers and make an ideal project for the beginner. The decorations are simple, having been adapted from other projects in the book, and can be flat or raised. The yo-yos, shown on page 109, are great fun especially when spinning, and would be a good project for children to try their hand at.

BLOOMS ON BROOMS

These wooden brooms were bought unvarnished and the strawberry and flower designs baked directly on to the broom head. They adhere firmly during the baking process. After painting the designs with water colours, the brooms were given two coats of yacht varnish and are now sturdy enough to be used regularly, or can be hung on the wall as decorative pieces if preferred.

DECORATED PLANT POTS

These pots have been painted with a deep brownish-pink emulsion and a lighter coloured trim.
The apples were baked on to the pots to get the curved shape for the terracotta pots but they did need to
be secured with PVA glue after baking. The dough stuck firmly to the wooden planter during baking without
any need for glue. To finish, the pots were sealed with two coats of satin polyurethane varnish.

LETTER RACK & CANDLE BOX

These two useful MDF pieces were painted in different shades of blue emulsion, leaving spaces for the dough decoration which adhered firmly during baking. The decorative motifs were taken from the sunflower and daisy designs on page 58, and the finished items were coated with two good coats of satin-finish polyurethane wood varnish.

EGG HOUSE & SALT BOX

The rather unusual distressed effect of the paintwork on these projects was achieved by painting first with a brick red emulsion, then with a second coat of dark green. When dry, the green was rubbed back with fine sandpaper to reveal the red underneath. The decoration with hen and vegetables is perfect for the kitchen.

MEMO BOARD & PLATE

This MDF blackboard and cheap papier mâché plate were painted with sunflower yellow emulsion and then sponged with a beige colour, leaving unpainted areas for decorating with the dough. The black area of the blackboard was masked off during painting. The decoration is quite flat, and leaves and flowers were cut with sugarcraft cutters for finer detail. After painting the dough, these two pieces were coated with the usual yacht varnish.

DESK SET

This three-piece desk set was painted first with emulsion, leaving bare the areas to be decorated, and was then adorned with a selection of farm animals. The pieces were purchased from 'Blankers' (see page 109) and would make a lovely gift for a man or for somebody who is studying, and could be decorated with anything you like.

WASTE BIN & MINI CHEST OF DRAWERS

These larger items look good decorated with dough and are most useful items. The drawers were taken out of the mini chest of drawers for baking, and the bin has dough on one side only. If you wished to decorate on all sides, you would have to bake each side individually. It won't hurt the already baked dough to go back into the oven.

TEMPLATES

These templates are for specific projects and are actual-size. Simply trace or photocopy the template on to thin card. Cut out the shape, lay lightly on top of the rolled out dough and cut around the outline using a sharp knife.

The templates may also be used to enlarge or reduce designs. In this case the template will need to be enlarged or reduced using a photocopier. Remember, of course, that dough requirements will also vary with the size of the model.

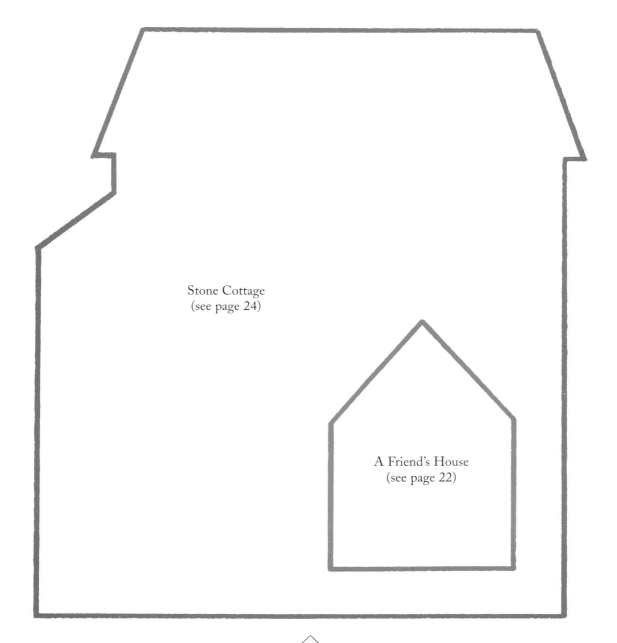

Stone Cottage
(see page 24)

A Friend's House
(see page 22)

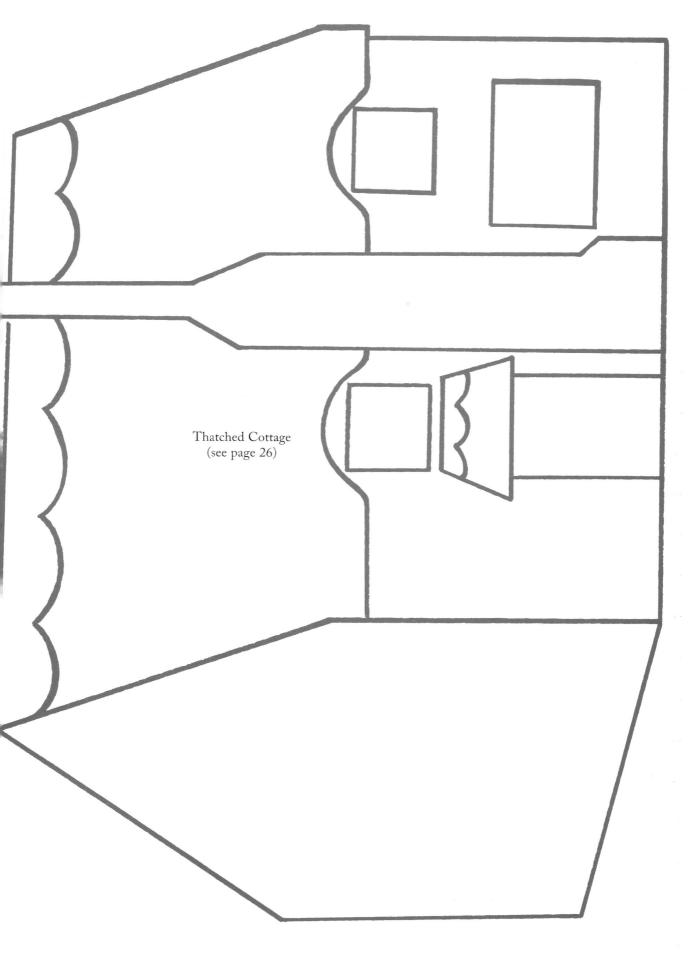

Thatched Cottage
(see page 26)

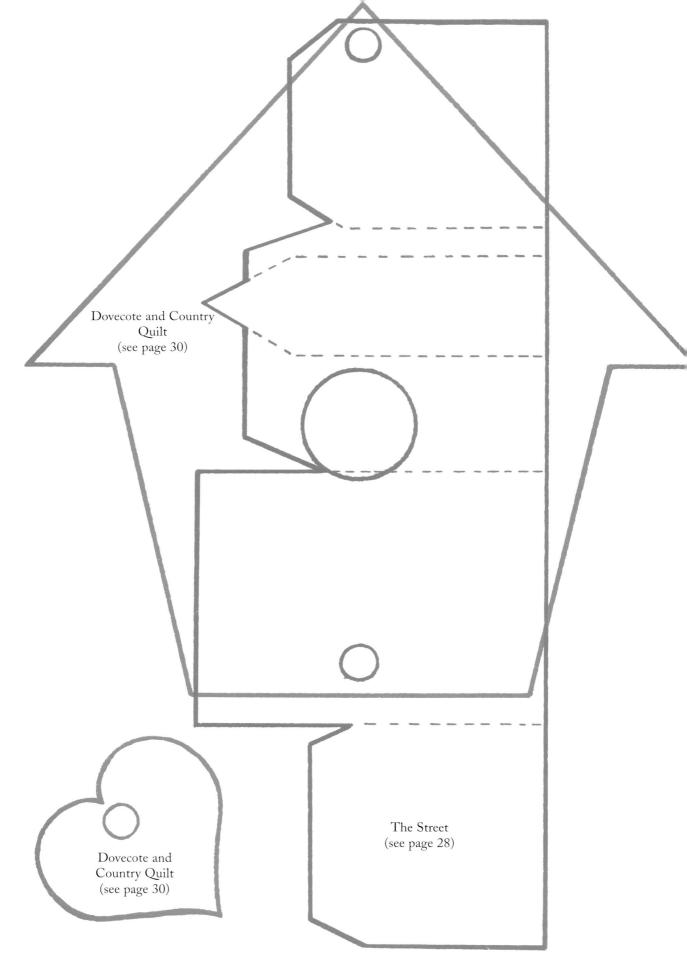

Dovecote and Country
Quilt
(see page 30)

Dovecote and
Country Quilt
(see page 30)

The Street
(see page 28)

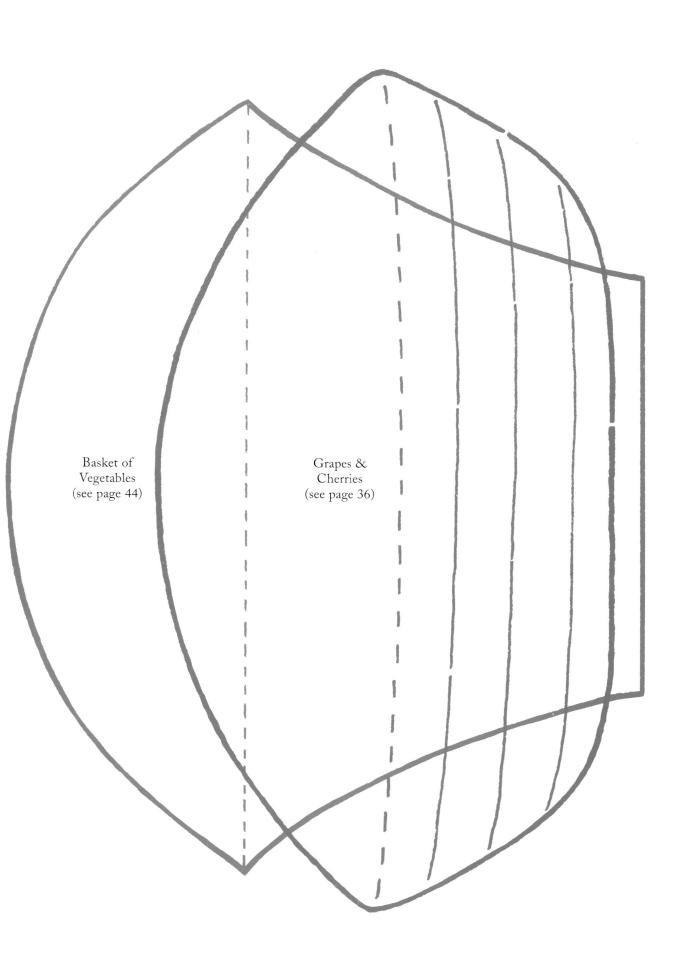

Basket of
Vegetables
(see page 44)

Grapes &
Cherries
(see page 36)

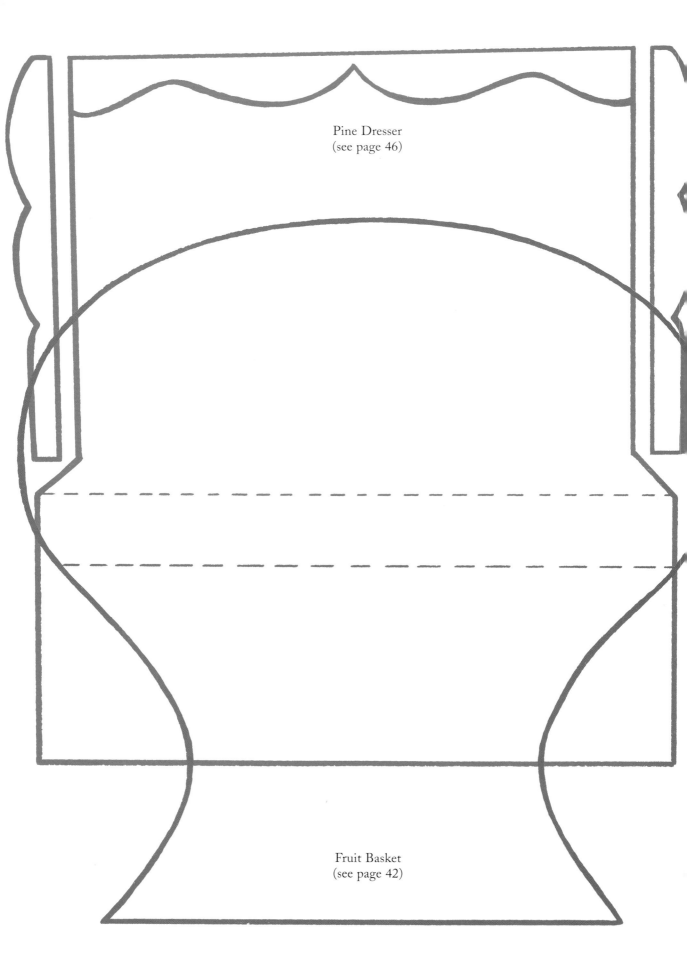

Pine Dresser
(see page 46)

Fruit Basket
(see page 42)

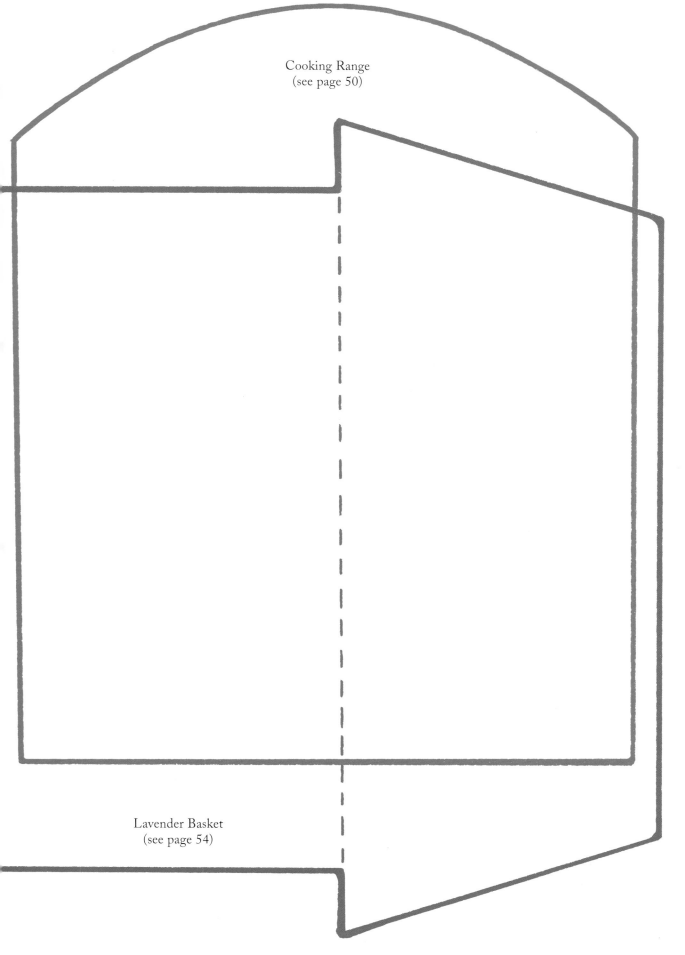

Cooking Range
(see page 50)

Lavender Basket
(see page 54)

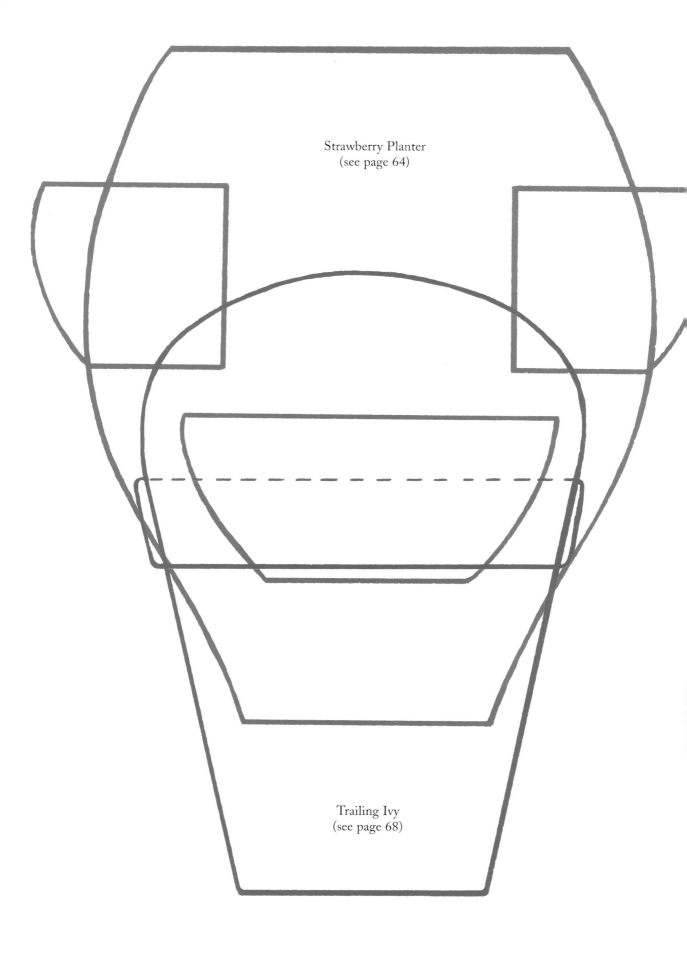

Strawberry Planter
(see page 64)

Trailing Ivy
(see page 68)

Basic Plaque
(see pages 86 and 92)

Rabbits With Heart
(see page 80)

Counting Sheep
(see page 82)

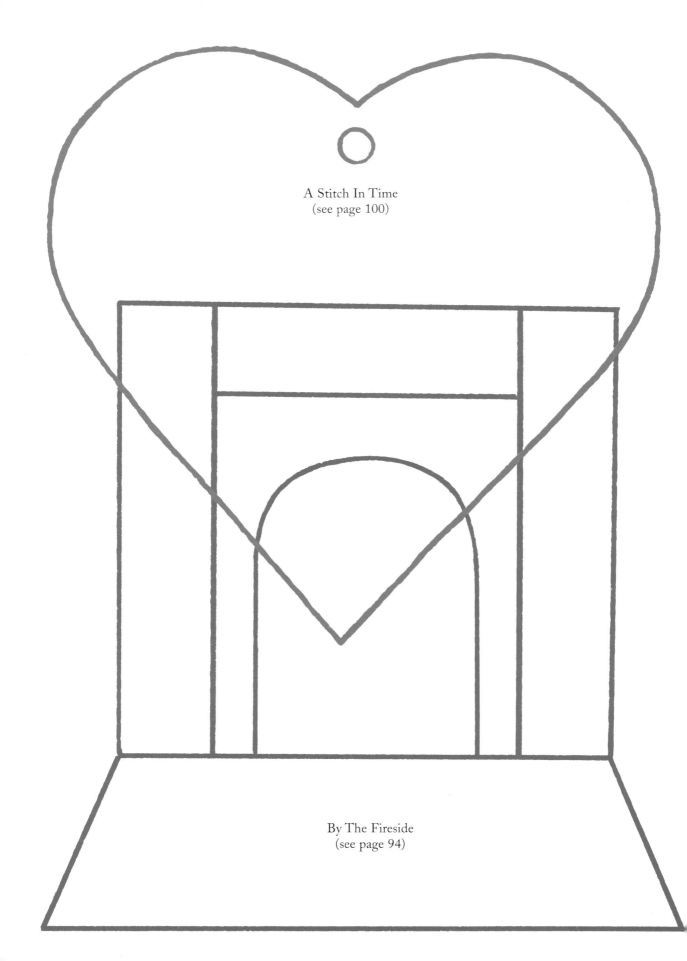

A Stitch In Time
(see page 100)

By The Fireside
(see page 94)

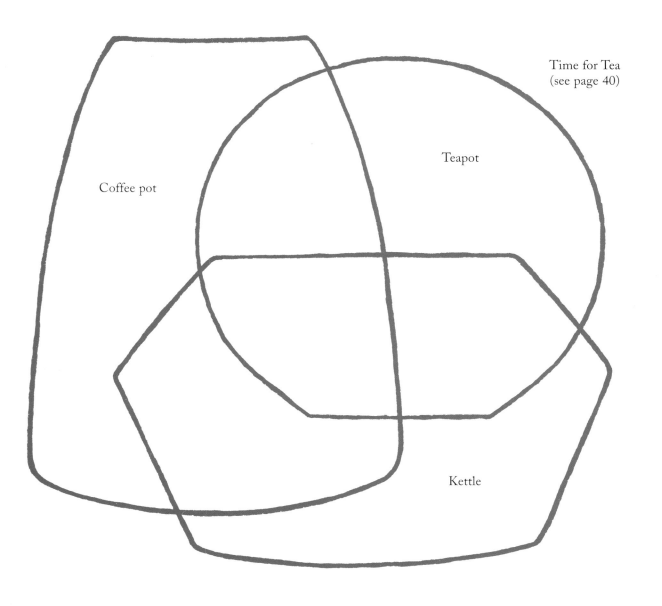

Coffee pot

Teapot

Time for Tea
(see page 40)

Kettle

ACKNOWLEDGEMENTS

My sincere thanks to the following people without whose help and support this book would not have been written.

My husband Ken for technical support and for varnishing all the projects in this book. My children, Kate and Emma, for their patience whilst I have been buried in a pile of paper and not giving them the attention they deserve. My parents, Mary and Mick Mallin, for just being there. Friends, Elizabeth and Victoria Cook, Linda Allen, Sarah Day, and Pam Marchant without whom my business would grind to a halt. Louise Dalby for her wonderful bathing beauties. Glenys and Roger Rowlett for the idea behind the 'Taking it Easy' project. Michael and Lisa Barnes of 'Blankers', Joan Cobb of Cotswold Village Crafts. Rosemary Stammers for introducing me to doughcraft. Jane Greenoff for inspiring me to write and my friend Chris Jones for always seeming to know instinctively when I needed some peace to work, and for amusing my children for hours on end!

Finally, I would like to thank photographers Paul and Pam Biddle for their superb work and everybody at David & Charles, in particular Cheryl Brown, Jane Trollope and Kay Ball for making the production of this book so enjoyable, and everybody in the publicity and sales office.

INDEX